WINNING WITH STOCKS

A Comprehensive Guide to Successful Investing

JACK FISHER

I0479257

Table of Contents

CHAPTER 1. INTRODUCTION TO STOCK INVESTING

"Over the long term, the stock market news will be good. In the 20th century, the United States endured two world wars and other traumatic and expensive military conflicts; the Depression; a dozen or so recessions and financial panics; oil shocks; a flu epidemic; and the resignation of a disgraced president. Yet the Dow rose from 66 to 11,497."

Warren Buffett

Investing in stocks is one of the most popular investment strategies used by individuals and institutions around the world. In simple terms, investing in stocks refers to the practice of buying shares in publicly traded companies, with the goal of earning a profit through capital appreciation or dividends.

One of the primary benefits of investing in stocks is the potential for high returns. Historically, stocks have provided higher returns than many other types of investments, such as bonds or savings accounts. Over the long term, stocks have generated an average annual return of around 10%, compared to just 3-5% for bonds and less than 1% for savings accounts. This higher return potential is one of the main reasons why many investors choose to invest in stocks.

The historic returns from stocks have been positive and offer higher potential returns than other investment options. Over the last 100 years, the US stock market, as measured by the S&P 500 index, has provided an average annual return of around 10%. However, the stock market's returns have varied significantly in different periods over the last century.

The early 1900s saw a period of significant growth for the US stock market. Between 1900 and 1925, the stock market experienced a compound annual growth rate of around 6.8%. However, this growth was followed by a period of significant volatility during the Great Depression, where the stock market lost around 80% of its value. It took until the 1950s for the stock market to recover to pre-Depression levels.

The post-World War II era saw a period of significant growth for the US stock market. Between 1946 and 1964, the stock market experienced a compound annual growth rate of around 16.5%. This growth was driven by a booming economy and technological advancements in industries such as aviation, electronics, and computers.

The 1970s and 1980s were a period of high inflation, energy crises, and economic turmoil, which resulted in a relatively flat stock market during this time. Between 1970 and 1981, the stock market experienced a compound annual growth rate of around 1.8%.

The 1990s saw a period of significant growth for the US stock market, fueled by the growth of the internet and technological advancements. Between 1990 and 1999, the stock market experienced a compound annual growth rate of around 18.2%.

The early 2000s saw a significant market correction and economic recession following the bursting of the dot-com bubble and the September 11th attacks. Between 2000 and 2009, the stock market experienced a compound annual growth rate of around -1.0%.

From 2010 to 2020, the US stock market experienced a compound annual growth rate of around 13.6%. This growth was driven by a strong economy, low-interest rates, and technological advancements in industries such as e-commerce and social media.

Another benefit of investing in stocks is the ability to diversify your portfolio. By investing in stocks from a variety of different companies and industries, you can spread out your risk and reduce the impact of any one company's poor performance. This can help to protect your investment and improve your overall returns.

Investing in stocks can also be a relatively easy and accessible investment strategy. Many online brokers and investment platforms offer low fees and minimum investment amounts, making it possible for even small investors to get started. Additionally, with the rise of robo-advisors and other automated investment tools, it is now easier than ever to create a diversified portfolio of stocks without needing to have extensive knowledge or experience in the stock market.

However, it is important to note that investing in stocks also carries risks. One of the main risks is the potential for volatility and fluctuations in the stock market. Prices can be affected by a wide range of factors, such as changes in the economy, geopolitical events, or company-specific news. This can lead to significant short-term losses and can make it difficult to predict the long-term performance of your investments.

Another risk is the potential for company-specific issues, such as poor management or unexpected competition, to impact the performance of your stocks. This is why it is important to research companies carefully before investing and to monitor your investments regularly.

Despite these risks, investing in stocks can be a valuable investment strategy for those who are willing to take on some risk in exchange for potentially higher returns. By diversifying your portfolio, staying informed about market trends, and investing for the long term, you can potentially generate significant wealth through stock investments.

CHAPTER 2.
UNDERSTANDING
THE STOCK MARKET

"In the short run, the market is a voting machine, but in the long run, it is a weighing machine."

Peter Lynch

At its most basic level, the stock market is a platform where companies issue and sell shares of their stock to investors. When you buy a share of stock, you are essentially buying a small piece of ownership in the company. This ownership comes with certain rights, such as the ability to vote on certain company matters and to receive a portion of the company's profits in the form of dividends.

The stock market is also a place where investors can buy and sell these shares of stock. Prices for individual stocks are determined by supply and demand, with buyers and sellers negotiating prices based on a range of factors, such as company performance, economic conditions, and investor sentiment.

There are two primary types of stock markets: the primary market and the secondary market. The primary market is where companies issue new shares of stock to raise capital. This typically happens through an initial public offering (IPO), where a company offers its shares to the public for the first time. Investors who participate in an IPO are typically looking to buy shares in a company that they believe has significant growth potential and will perform well in the future.

The secondary market is where most trading in stocks occurs. This is where investors buy and sell existing shares of stock that have already been issued. The most well-known example of a secondary market is the New York Stock Exchange (NYSE), which is where many of the world's largest companies trade their shares. Stock exchanges help to ensure that trades are executed in a fair and efficient manner, with rules and regulations in place to prevent insider trading or other forms of market manipulation. Market makers help to ensure that there is liquidity in the market by buying and selling shares of stock on a regular basis. Market makers are typically large financial institutions that have the resources and expertise to trade stocks in large volumes.

To facilitate trading in the secondary market, there are a number of different players involved. The most well-known are brokers, who act as intermediaries between buyers and sellers. Brokers can be individuals or large investment firms, and they typically charge a commission or fee for their services.

Indices are typically calculated using a weighted average of the prices of a group of stocks. This means that stocks with a higher market capitalization or higher trading volume have a greater impact on the index than smaller or less traded stocks. Some of the most well-known indices include the S&P 500, which tracks the performance of 500 large-cap US companies, and the Dow Jones Industrial Average, which tracks the performance of 30 blue-chip US companies.

One of the key benefits of using indices to track stock price movements is that they provide a way to measure the overall health and direction of the stock market. For example, if an index is trending upwards, it can indicate that investors are bullish on the market and expect prices to continue rising. Conversely, if an index is trending downwards, it can suggest that investors are bearish on the market and expect prices to fall.

Indices can also be used to make informed investment decisions. For example, investors may use an index to track the performance of a particular sector, such as technology or healthcare, and make investment decisions based on trends and patterns in that sector. Additionally, indices can be used to track the performance of a particular country's stock market or the global stock market as a whole, providing investors with a broad view of the investment landscape.

Stock price movements, on the other hand, are driven by a wide range of factors, including company performance, market trends, economic indicators, and geopolitical events. These factors can cause stock prices to fluctuate rapidly and unpredictably, making it difficult for investors to accurately predict price movements.

One of the most important drivers of stock price movements is company performance. If a company reports strong earnings or announces a new product or service, its stock price may rise as investors become more optimistic about the company's future prospects. Conversely, if a company reports weak earnings or experiences a setback, its stock price may fall as investors become more pessimistic.

Market trends and economic indicators can also play a significant role in driving stock price movements. For example, if interest rates rise, it can cause investors to become more cautious and may lead to a downturn in the stock market. Similarly, if a country experiences an economic recession, it can lead to a broader downturn in the stock market as investors become more risk-averse. Here some of the most significant recessions experienced by different countries over the years:

1. The Great Depression (1929-1939) - United States of America: The Great Depression is one of the most

severe and prolonged economic recessions in history. Triggered by the stock market crash of 1929, the depression saw a significant decrease in GDP, rising unemployment, and a decline in the standard of living for many Americans. It took until the start of World War II for the US economy to fully recover.

2. The Oil Crisis (1973-1975) - Worldwide: The Oil Crisis of 1973 was a period of economic recession that was triggered by the Arab-Israeli War in October 1973. As a result of the war, several Arab oil-producing nations embargoed oil shipments to countries that supported Israel, causing a sharp rise in oil prices. This led to a global economic recession, with many countries experiencing high inflation, rising unemployment, and decreased economic growth. The recession lasted until 1975 when oil prices stabilized and economies began to recover.

3. The Lost Decade (1991-2000) - Japan: Japan's Lost Decade was a period of economic stagnation that lasted from the early 1990s until the early 2000s. The recession was caused by a bursting of a real estate and asset bubble, leading to a decline in consumer and business spending. The economy experienced several years of negative GDP growth, deflation, and rising unemployment, which impacted Japan's economy for years to come.

4. The Asian Financial Crisis (1997-1998) - Several countries in Asia: The Asian Financial Crisis was a period of economic turmoil that affected several countries in Asia, including Thailand, Indonesia, South Korea, and Malaysia. The crisis was caused by a combination of factors, including high levels of foreign debt and overinvestment in real estate and other speculative ventures. The crisis led to a sharp

decline in GDP growth, rising unemployment, and social unrest.

5. The European Sovereign Debt Crisis (2009-2013) - Several countries in Europe: The European Sovereign Debt Crisis was a period of economic turmoil that affected several countries in Europe, including Greece, Portugal, Spain, and Italy. The crisis was caused by a combination of factors, including high levels of public debt, weak banking systems, and a lack of fiscal coordination between European countries. The crisis led to a sharp decline in GDP growth, rising unemployment, and social unrest.

CHAPTER 3.
BUILDING A WINNING
PORTFOLIO

"The four most dangerous words in investing are: this time it's different."

John Templeton

Building a diversified portfolio of stocks is an essential part of any successful investment strategy. By diversifying your portfolio, you can minimize risk and potentially maximize returns by investing in a range of different stocks and industries.

The first step in building a diversified portfolio is to identify your investment goals and risk tolerance. Your investment goals may include factors such as income generation, capital appreciation, or a combination of both. Your risk tolerance will depend on your age, financial situation, and investment experience. Once you have established your goals and risk tolerance, you can begin to select stocks that fit your investment criteria.

The next step is to determine the appropriate asset allocation for your portfolio. This involves deciding how much of your portfolio should be invested in stocks, bonds, and other asset classes. The general rule of thumb is that younger investors can afford to take more risk and should have a higher allocation to stocks, while older investors should have a higher allocation to bonds and other fixed-income securities.

The 60-40 division between stocks and bonds is a common strategy used by many investors to balance their portfolios. The strategy involves investing 60% of the portfolio in stocks and 40% in bonds. The allocation is based on the belief that stocks provide higher returns but also carry higher risks, while bonds provide lower returns but also lower risks.

One of the primary advantages of the 60-40 division strategy is that it provides a good balance between growth and stability. Stocks have historically provided higher returns than bonds, and investing 60% of the portfolio in stocks can help investors achieve higher long-term growth. However, stocks are also more volatile and carry higher risks, so having 40% of the portfolio in bonds can provide a cushion against market downturns and help preserve capital.

Another advantage of the 60-40 division strategy is that it is relatively simple to implement and maintain. Investors can easily rebalance their portfolios by buying and selling stocks and bonds as needed to maintain the desired allocation. This can help reduce transaction costs and make it easier for investors to stick to their investment plan.

However, there are also some potential disadvantages to the 60-40 division strategy. One of the main disadvantages is that it may not be appropriate for all investors. For example, younger investors with a longer investment horizon may be better suited for a more aggressive allocation, such as 80% stocks and 20% bonds, in order to maximize long-term growth. On the other hand, older investors who are closer to retirement may prefer a more conservative allocation, such as 40% stocks and 60% bonds, in order to minimize risk and preserve capital.

Another potential disadvantage of the 60-40 division strategy is that it may not provide adequate diversification. While stocks and bonds are different asset classes, they are still both subject to market risks, such as interest rate changes, inflation, and economic downturns. Investors may want to consider adding other asset classes to their portfolios, such as real estate, commodities, or alternative investments, to further diversify their holdings and reduce risk.

When implementing the 60-40 division strategy, there are several factors to consider. First, investors should consider their investment goals, risk tolerance, and time horizon. Investors with a longer time horizon and higher risk tolerance may be more comfortable with a higher allocation to stocks, while those with a shorter time horizon and lower risk tolerance may prefer a higher allocation to bonds.

Second, investors should consider the current market environment and economic conditions. For example, in a low-interest-rate environment, bonds may provide lower returns and be less attractive to investors. In this case, investors may want to consider reducing their bond allocation and increasing their stock allocation.

Once you have determined your asset allocation, you can begin selecting individual stocks for your portfolio. It is important to select stocks from a variety of industries and sectors to reduce risk. For example, you may want to include stocks from sectors such as technology, healthcare, finance, and consumer goods. You should also consider investing in both large-cap and small-cap stocks to further diversify your portfolio.

Another important factor to consider when building a diversified portfolio of stocks is to avoid overconcentration in any one stock or sector. This means that you should limit your exposure to any single stock or industry to avoid being overly impacted by any one company's performance. A good rule of thumb is to limit your exposure to any single stock to no more than 10% of your portfolio.

Warren Buffett, the legendary investor and CEO of Berkshire Hathaway, is widely known for his success in the stock market. Over the years, he has offered numerous insights into his investment philosophy, and one of the most famous of these is his belief that you don't need more than six stocks to have a diversified portfolio.

At first glance, this may seem like a surprising statement. After all, conventional wisdom would suggest that in order to reduce risk and increase returns, investors should hold a wide range of stocks from different industries and sectors. However, Buffett's reasoning is based on a deeper understanding of what true diversification means.

For Buffett, the key to diversification is not simply owning a large number of stocks, but rather owning a carefully chosen selection of high-quality companies with strong competitive advantages and stable long-term growth prospects. By focusing on these companies, investors can reduce their exposure to market volatility and benefit from the compounding power of high-quality businesses over time.

Of course, selecting just six stocks requires careful consideration and research. Buffett has famously emphasized the importance of investing in companies with "economic moats" - that is, businesses with sustainable competitive advantages that allow them to maintain their market position and generate strong profits over the long term. He also looks for companies with strong management teams, solid financials, and a proven track record of growth and innovation.

In addition to selecting individual stocks, you may also want to consider investing in index funds or exchange-traded funds (ETFs) that track broad market indices such as the S&P 500 or the Dow Jones Industrial Average. These funds provide exposure to a range of different stocks and industries and can be an effective way to achieve diversification without the need for individual stock selection.

Analyzing companies is a crucial skill for investors, whether they are seasoned professionals or individual investors. By carefully examining a company's financial statements, management, industry trends, and other factors, investors can gain insight into the company's strengths and weaknesses, and make informed decisions about whether to invest in the company. Here are some key steps to follow when analyzing a company:

1. Understand the company's industry and market position: Before analyzing a company's financials, it's important to have a good understanding of the industry in which the company operates. This includes the size of the market, the key competitors, and any trends or challenges facing the industry. It's also important to understand the company's position within the industry and how it differentiates itself from its competitors.

2. Review the company's financial statements: The most important source of information about a company's financial performance is its financial statements. This includes the income statement, balance sheet, and cash flow statement. These documents provide information about the company's revenue, expenses, assets, liabilities, and cash flow over a specific period of time. Investors should review these statements carefully to get a sense of the company's financial health and performance.

3. Evaluate the company's management team: A company's management team plays a critical role in its success or failure. Investors should evaluate the CEO and other top executives to understand their track record, leadership style, and overall vision for the company. It's also important to assess the

company's board of directors and any governance structures in place.

4. Consider the company's competitive advantages: Companies that have strong competitive advantages are more likely to succeed over the long term. These advantages might include a proprietary technology, a well-known brand, or a unique distribution network. Investors should consider whether the company has any such advantages and how sustainable they are over time.

5. Assess the company's growth potential: Investors should consider whether the company has potential for growth in the future. This might include expanding into new markets or product lines, developing new technology, or pursuing other strategic initiatives. Investors should also evaluate the company's track record of growth and how well it has executed on previous growth initiatives.

6. Consider any risks or challenges facing the company: No company is without risk, and investors should consider any potential risks or challenges that could impact the company's performance. This might include factors such as changes in regulations, shifts in consumer preferences, or increasing competition from other companies.

Analyzing industries and sectors is an important skill for investors who are looking to build a well-diversified portfolio. By understanding the trends, challenges, and opportunities facing different industries and sectors, investors can make informed decisions about where to allocate their capital. Here are some key steps to follow when analyzing industries and sectors:

1. Understand the macroeconomic environment: The

first step in analyzing industries and sectors is to get a sense of the macroeconomic environment. This includes factors such as interest rates, inflation, and GDP growth. These macroeconomic factors can have a significant impact on different industries and sectors, and investors should be aware of how they might impact their investments.

2. Identify the key players in the industry or sector: Once you have a sense of the macroeconomic environment, you can begin to look at specific industries and sectors. Identify the key players in the industry or sector, including the largest companies and any emerging players. This will give you a sense of the competitive landscape and how the industry or sector is evolving over time.

3. Assess the industry or sector's growth potential: Consider the long-term growth potential of the industry or sector. This might include factors such as demographic trends, technological innovations, or changes in consumer behavior. Investors should also evaluate any potential risks or challenges facing the industry or sector, such as changing regulations or disruptive new entrants.

4. Evaluate the financial performance of companies in the industry or sector: Investors should evaluate the financial performance of companies in the industry or sector, including factors such as revenue growth, profitability, and cash flow. This will give you a sense of how individual companies are performing within the broader industry or sector.

5. Consider the valuation of companies in the industry or sector: Finally, investors should consider the valuation of companies in the industry or sector.

This might include factors such as price-to-earnings ratios, price-to-sales ratios, or other valuation metrics. By comparing the valuation of different companies within the same industry or sector, investors can identify opportunities for potential investment.

Portfolio management software is a valuable tool for investors looking to manage their investments and track their performance. These tools can help investors make informed decisions about asset allocation, risk management, and overall portfolio strategy. Some of the key features of portfolio management software include:

1. Portfolio tracking: These tools allow investors to track their investments across different asset classes, including stocks, bonds, mutual funds, and ETFs. Many portfolio management software options allow you to import data from your brokerage account, making it easy to get started.

2. Performance analysis: Portfolio management software provides detailed analytics and reporting features that allow investors to track the performance of their investments over time. Many tools also offer benchmarking features, allowing you to compare your portfolio's performance to other indices or metrics.

3. Asset allocation: These tools can help investors optimize their asset allocation, ensuring that their portfolio is balanced and aligned with their investment goals. Some portfolio management software options offer asset allocation recommendations based on your investment objectives and risk tolerance.

4. Risk management: Portfolio management software can help investors assess the risk profile of their investments and make informed decisions about risk management. Some tools provide risk analysis tools, such as value-at-risk (VaR) calculations or stress tests, to help investors evaluate potential losses in different market scenarios.

5. Trading: Some portfolio management software options also offer trading features, allowing investors to buy and sell assets directly from the platform. These tools can provide a seamless trading experience and can help investors execute trades more efficiently.

Some of the most popular portfolio management software options include:

1. Morningstar Portfolio Manager: Morningstar is a well-known financial research firm that offers a range of portfolio management tools. Their Portfolio Manager allows investors to track their investments, analyze performance, and evaluate risk.

2. Personal Capital: Personal Capital is a comprehensive financial management tool that includes portfolio management features. This tool allows investors to track their investments, monitor their net worth, and plan for retirement.

3. Betterment: Betterment is a robo-advisor that provides automated portfolio management services. Their platform uses algorithms to manage your investments and optimize your asset allocation.

Here are some key steps to follow when using portfolio management software:

1. Set up your portfolio: The first step in using portfolio management software is to set up your portfolio. This might include entering information about the assets you own, such as stocks, bonds, mutual funds, or ETFs. Many portfolio management tools allow you to import data from your brokerage account, making it easy to get started.

2. Set your investment goals: Once your portfolio is set up, you can begin to think about your investment goals. Are you investing for retirement, saving for a down payment on a home, or looking to generate income? By setting specific investment goals, you can use portfolio management software to help you stay on track.

3. Monitor your portfolio performance: One of the key benefits of portfolio management software is the ability to track the performance of your investments over time. Many tools offer detailed analytics and reporting features that allow you to see how your portfolio is performing relative to benchmarks or other metrics.

4. Rebalance your portfolio: As your investments grow and change over time, it's important to periodically rebalance your portfolio to maintain your desired asset allocation. Portfolio management software can help you identify when it's time to buy or sell assets to stay aligned with your investment goals.

5. Evaluate risk: Another important feature of portfolio management software is the ability to evaluate risk.

By assessing the risk profile of your investments, you can make informed decisions about how to manage risk and minimize potential losses.

6. Stay informed: Finally, it's important to stay informed about market trends, news, and other factors that could impact your investments. Many portfolio management tools offer real-time news and analysis features that can help you stay up to date and make informed decisions about your portfolio.

CHAPTER 4.
STRATEGIES FOR SUCCESSFUL STOCK INVESTING

"The intelligent investor is a realist who sells to optimists and buys from pessimists."

Benjamin Graham

Investing in the stock market can be a daunting task, with numerous strategies and approaches to choose from. Each strategy has its own set of advantages and disadvantages, and investors need to carefully consider their investment goals and risk tolerance before deciding which strategy to pursue. In this chapter, we will explore the key principles, benefits, and drawbacks of these three investment strategies to help you make informed decisions when investing in the stock market.

Value investing is a strategy that seeks to identify undervalued stocks in the market. The basic idea is to look for stocks that are trading at a discount to their intrinsic value. Value investors typically use fundamental analysis to evaluate a company's financial health and growth potential, and look for stocks that have a low price-to-earnings (P/E) ratio, low price-to-book (P/B) ratio, and high dividend yield. Famous value investors include Warren Buffett and Benjamin Graham. Like any investment strategy, value investing has its advantages and disadvantages.

Advantages:

1. Potential for high returns: By buying undervalued stocks and holding them until they increase in value, value investors have the potential to earn high returns.

2. Focus on fundamentals: Value investors focus on a company's underlying fundamentals, such as its earnings, assets, and cash flow. This approach can help investors identify companies with strong financials that may be undervalued by the market.

3. Margin of safety: Value investing emphasizes the importance of having a margin of safety when buying stocks. By buying stocks at a discount, value investors are able to minimize their downside risk and potentially increase their upside potential.

4. Contrarian approach: Value investing involves taking a contrarian approach to investing, which means buying stocks when others are selling. This can provide opportunities to buy quality companies at a discount.

Disadvantages:

1. Long-term approach: Value investing is a long-term investment strategy that requires patience and discipline. It can take time for the market to recognize the true value of a company, so value investors need to be willing to hold onto their investments for extended periods of time.

2. Limited upside potential: While value investing has the potential for high returns, it also has limited upside potential. Value investors are typically looking for companies that are undervalued by the market, which means they may not have the same growth potential as other stocks.

3. Value traps: Sometimes, stocks are undervalued for a reason. These companies may have fundamental issues that make it difficult for them to increase their value over time. Value investors need to be careful to avoid falling into the trap of buying stocks that may not be able to increase in value.

4. Limited diversification: Because value investing involves selecting individual stocks, it can be difficult to achieve diversification. This means that value investors need to carefully select a portfolio of stocks that are diversified across different sectors and industries to minimize their risk.

Growth investing is a strategy that involves looking for stocks with high growth potential. These companies typically have strong earnings growth, a large addressable market, and a competitive advantage over their peers. Investors using this strategy are willing to pay a premium for these stocks in the hopes of generating outsized returns over the long-term. Some famous growth investors include Peter Lynch and Thomas Rowe Price.

Advantages:

1. Potential for high returns: Growth stocks are often companies that are experiencing rapid growth and are expected to continue to grow at a fast pace. This can provide investors with the potential for high returns.

2. Strong market performance: In general, growth stocks tend to outperform the broader market, particularly during periods of economic growth.

3. Focus on innovation: Growth companies are often at the forefront of innovation in their industries, which can lead to new products and services that can create significant value for investors.

4. Diversification: Growth investing can provide investors with the opportunity to diversify their portfolio across different sectors and industries. This can help to reduce overall risk.

Disadvantages:

1. High valuations: Growth stocks are often priced at a premium compared to the broader market, which can make them more vulnerable to market fluctuations.

2. High risk: Growth companies are often in the early stages of their development, which means they are subject to a higher degree of risk than more established companies.

3. Limited dividend payments: Many growth companies reinvest their profits into their business rather than paying dividends to shareholders, which can limit the potential for income.

4. Uncertainty: Because growth companies are often in the early stages of their development, there is a high degree of uncertainty about their future prospects. This can make it difficult for investors to accurately predict future earnings and growth potential.

Income investing is a strategy that involves focusing on stocks with high dividend yields. These companies typically have stable cash flows and a history of paying dividends to their shareholders. The goal is to generate a steady stream of income from these stocks while also benefiting from potential capital appreciation over time. Famous income investors include John Paulson and Howard Marks.

Advantages:

1. Potential for income: Dividend-paying stocks can provide investors with a regular income stream, which can be particularly attractive for those who are looking to supplement their retirement savings or generate passive income.

2. Stable returns: Dividend-paying stocks are often companies that have a long track record of stability and profitability. This can provide investors with more predictable returns over time.

3. Lower volatility: Dividend-paying stocks are often less volatile than other types of stocks, which can help to reduce overall portfolio risk.

4. Potential for long-term growth: Many dividend-paying companies are well-established and have a strong history of growth. This can provide investors with the potential for long-term growth as well as income.

Disadvantages:

1. Limited growth potential: Dividend-paying companies may be more focused on paying dividends to shareholders than reinvesting profits into their business. This can limit their potential for growth and may not be ideal for investors who are looking for high-growth investments.

2. Vulnerability to economic downturns: Dividend-paying companies may be more vulnerable to economic downturns, as they may have less cash available to reinvest in their business during tough times.

3. Potential for dividend cuts: Companies can cut or eliminate dividends at any time, which can be a risk for investors who are relying on dividend income.

4. Limited diversification: Many dividend-paying companies are concentrated in certain sectors, which can limit the diversification potential of a portfolio.

Momentum investing is a strategy that involves looking for stocks that have strong recent performance. Investors using this strategy believe that stocks that have been performing well recently are likely to continue to do so in the near-term. The goal is to buy these stocks and sell them once their momentum starts to slow down. Famous momentum investors include Mark Minervini and James O'Shaughnessy.

Advantages:

1. Potential for high returns: Momentum stocks can have significant short-term gains and potentially outperform other investment strategies.

2. Clear entry and exit signals: Momentum investors use technical analysis to identify stocks that are trending and enter and exit positions based on signals.

3. Simple to implement: The momentum strategy is simple and easy to implement, making it accessible to a wide range of investors.

4. Risk management: Momentum investors use stop-loss orders to limit losses and reduce risk.

Disadvantages:

1. High volatility: Momentum stocks can be highly volatile and subject to significant price swings, which can lead to large losses if positions are not managed properly.

2. Short-term focus: Momentum investing is focused on short-term gains and can result in missed opportunities for long-term growth.

3. Overcrowding: The popularity of momentum investing can lead to overcrowding in certain stocks or sectors, which can increase risk and limit potential returns.

4. Potential for market timing mistakes: Momentum investing requires precise market timing, which can be difficult to achieve consistently.

Index investing is a strategy that involves investing in a diversified portfolio of stocks that track a particular index, such as the S&P 500 or the NASDAQ. This strategy is popular among investors who want to achieve broad market exposure and minimize the risk of individual stock picking. Index funds are typically low-cost and provide investors with instant diversification. Famous proponents of index investing include Jack Bogle and Burton Malkiel.

Advantages:

1. Low cost: Index funds have low expense ratios compared to actively managed funds, which can result in higher returns for investors over the long-term.

2. Diversification: Index funds offer broad market

exposure and diversification across different sectors, which can help reduce risk.

3. Consistent returns: Since index funds track a market index, they tend to provide consistent returns over time.

4. Accessibility: Index funds are easy to purchase and can be bought through a variety of platforms, including online brokers and robo-advisors.

Disadvantages:

1. Limited upside potential: Index funds are designed to track a market index, so their returns will generally be in line with the overall market, which can limit potential upside.

2. No flexibility: Index funds cannot deviate from their benchmark index, so they may miss out on opportunities to invest in high-performing companies or sectors.

3. Inefficient tax management: Index funds may generate taxable gains when the index they track changes or when there are changes in the composition of the fund.

4. Exposure to market fluctuations: Index funds are subject to market fluctuations and can experience losses during market downturns.

Index funds are a type of mutual fund that invests in a diversified portfolio of stocks or other securities that closely tracks the performance of a market index. Unlike actively managed funds that aim to outperform the market, index funds are designed to match the returns of a particular index, such as the S&P 500 or the

Nasdaq Composite.

The concept of index funds was pioneered by Jack Bogle, the founder of Vanguard Group, in the 1970s. Bogle saw that most actively managed funds underperformed their benchmarks over the long term due to high fees and expenses. He believed that investors would be better served by a low-cost, passive investment strategy that simply aimed to match the market's returns.

Bogle's vision became a reality in 1976 with the launch of the first index fund, the Vanguard 500 Index Fund. The fund tracked the performance of the S&P 500, the most widely followed index of large-cap U.S. stocks, and charged an expense ratio of just 0.16%, far lower than the industry average. The fund was an immediate success, attracting investors who wanted a low-cost way to invest in the stock market.

Warren Buffett, the legendary investor and CEO of Berkshire Hathaway, was an early proponent of index funds. In his annual letter to shareholders in 1990, Buffett famously declared that "a low-cost index fund is the most sensible equity investment for the great majority of investors."

Buffett's endorsement of index funds was based on his belief that most active investors, including professional fund managers, would fail to beat the market over the long term. He argued that the fees and expenses charged by active managers ate into returns and that their stock-picking skills were no better than random chance. Buffett believed that index funds offered a simple and effective way for investors to participate in the stock market without taking on the risks of active management.

Both Bogle and Buffett were proven right over the years as index funds gained in popularity and outperformed most actively managed funds. According to Morningstar, over the 10-year period ending in 2020, 85% of U.S. large-cap equity funds underperformed their benchmarks, while the Vanguard 500 Index Fund delivered an annualized return of 13.9%, outpacing

90% of its actively managed peers.

CHAPTER 5.
ANALYZING FINANCIAL STATEMENTS

"Accounting is the language of business. You have to know the language to understand what you're reading in financial statements."

Warren Buffett

Financial statement analysis involves examining a company's financial statements, including the balance sheet, income statement, and cash flow statement, in order to evaluate its financial health. This process can reveal important information about a company's assets, liabilities, revenue, and expenses, which can help investors determine whether the company is a good investment.

One of the main benefits of financial statement analysis is that it can help investors identify companies that are undervalued or overvalued. By examining a company's financial statements, investors can compare its financial performance to that of its peers and industry benchmarks. This can reveal whether a company is generating strong profits and cash flow relative to its competitors, or whether it is struggling to keep up.

Another important benefit of financial statement analysis is that it can help investors identify potential red flags or warning signs. For example, if a company has a high level of debt or is consistently losing money, this may indicate that it is not a good investment. By identifying these warning signs early on, investors can avoid making costly mistakes.

However, it's important to note that financial statement analysis is not foolproof. Companies can manipulate their financial statements in order to make themselves appear more profitable or healthy than they actually are. For this reason, it's important for investors to use multiple sources of information when evaluating a company, including news articles, industry reports, and expert opinions.

To properly analyze a financial statement, start by examining the balance sheet. Analyzing the balance sheet of a company is an important step in the process of evaluating a potential investment opportunity. The balance sheet is a financial statement that provides a snapshot of a company's financial health at a specific point in time. It presents a detailed breakdown of the company's assets, liabilities, and equity, and provides investors with a wealth of information that can be used to make informed investment decisions.

One of the main benefits of analyzing the balance sheet is that it allows investors to assess a company's financial stability. By examining a company's assets and liabilities, investors can determine whether the company has sufficient resources to meet its financial obligations, such as debt payments or operating expenses. This can help investors avoid companies that may be at risk of bankruptcy or financial distress.

Another important aspect of the balance sheet is that it can provide insight into a company's capital structure. By analyzing the composition of a company's equity and debt, investors can determine how much financial leverage the company is using to fund its operations. This can help investors determine whether a company is taking on too much debt, which can increase its financial risk and potentially lead to default or bankruptcy.

In addition to evaluating a company's financial stability and capital structure, the balance sheet can also provide information about a company's financial performance. For example, by examining changes in the company's assets and liabilities over time, investors can determine whether the company is growing or shrinking. They can also identify trends in the company's financial performance, such as increasing or decreasing profitability. Here are the main parameters to look for in a balance sheet analysis:

1. Current Assets: Current assets are assets that can be converted into cash within one year. Examples include cash and cash equivalents, accounts receivable, and inventory. Analyze trends in current assets to understand a company's liquidity.

2. Non-Current Assets: Non-current assets are assets that cannot be easily converted into cash and have a useful life of more than one year. Examples include property, plant, and equipment, and intangible assets. Analyze trends in non-current assets to understand a company's long-term investment strategy.

3. Current Liabilities: Current liabilities are debts that must be paid within one year. Examples include accounts payable, short-term loans, and accrued expenses. Analyze trends in current liabilities to understand a company's short-term liquidity and ability to meet its financial obligations.

4. Long-Term Liabilities: Long-term liabilities are debts that are due beyond one year. Examples include long-term loans and bonds. Analyze trends in long-term liabilities to understand a company's long-term debt management and leverage.

5. Equity: Equity represents the residual value of a company after its liabilities have been subtracted from its assets. Analyze trends in equity to understand a company's financial health and stability.

6. Working Capital: Working capital is calculated as current assets minus current liabilities. A positive working capital indicates a company has enough short-term assets to cover its short-term debts. Analyze trends in working capital to understand a company's liquidity and financial stability.

7. Debt-to-Equity Ratio: The debt-to-equity ratio is calculated as total debt divided by total equity. This ratio provides insights into a company's financial leverage and risk.

Next, move on to the income statement. Analyzing the income statement of a company is an important step in the process of evaluating a potential investment opportunity. The income statement, also known as the profit and loss statement, provides a summary of a company's revenues, expenses, and profits over a specific period of time. It is a valuable tool for investors who want to understand how a company is generating its revenue and whether it is profitable.

One of the main benefits of analyzing the income statement is that it allows investors to assess a company's revenue growth and profitability. By examining the company's revenues and expenses, investors can determine whether the company is generating enough revenue to cover its costs and generate a profit. This information can be used to evaluate a company's overall financial health and to determine whether it is a good investment opportunity.

Another important aspect of the income statement is that it can provide insight into a company's operational efficiency. By examining the company's cost of goods sold, gross profit margin, and operating expenses, investors can determine how efficiently the company is managing its operations. This can help investors identify potential areas for improvement, such as reducing costs or increasing efficiency, that could lead to higher profitability in the future.

In addition to evaluating a company's revenue growth, profitability, and operational efficiency, the income statement can also provide information about a company's earnings quality. By examining the company's net income and earnings per share, investors can determine how much of the company's earnings are attributable to ongoing operations versus one-time events or accounting adjustments. This can help investors identify potential risks or inconsistencies in a company's financial reporting. Here are the main parameters to look for in an income statement analysis:

1. Revenue: The first line of the income statement is revenue, which represents the total amount of money a company earned during the period. Look for trends in revenue growth over time and compare revenue to industry benchmarks.

2. Gross Profit: Gross profit is the difference between revenue and the cost of goods sold. Analyzing gross profit margins can provide insights into a company's pricing power and cost management.

3. Operating Expenses: Operating expenses include selling, general, and administrative expenses, research and development costs, and other expenses related to running the business. Analyze trends in operating expenses and compare them to industry benchmarks.

4. Operating Income: Operating income is the amount of profit a company earns from its operations before interest and taxes. Analyze trends in operating income and compare them to industry benchmarks.

5. Net Income: Net income is the amount of profit a company earns after all expenses are subtracted. Analyze trends in net income and compare them to industry benchmarks.

6. Earnings Per Share: Earnings per share (EPS) is the amount of net income a company earns per share of its outstanding stock. Analyze trends in EPS and compare them to industry benchmarks.

7. Other Key Metrics: Other key metrics to consider include return on equity (ROE), return on assets (ROA), and profit margins. Analyze these metrics to gain insights into a company's profitability and efficiency.

Finally, examine the cash flow statement. Analyzing the cash flow statement of a company is an important step in the process of evaluating a potential investment opportunity. The cash flow statement provides a summary of a company's inflows and outflows of cash over a specific period of time. It is a valuable tool for investors who want to understand how a company is generating and using its cash, and whether it is generating enough cash to support its operations and growth.

One of the main benefits of analyzing the cash flow statement is that it allows investors to assess a company's cash generation and management. By examining the company's operating cash flow, investors can determine how much cash the company is generating from its core operations. This information can be used to evaluate the company's ability to fund its operations and to pay dividends or invest in future growth opportunities.

Another important aspect of the cash flow statement is that it can provide insight into a company's capital expenditures and financing activities. By examining the company's investing and financing cash flows, investors can determine how much cash the company is spending on capital expenditures, such as property, plant, and equipment, and how much cash it is raising through debt or equity financing. This information can be used to evaluate the company's capital structure and to determine whether it is using its cash effectively to support its growth.

In addition to evaluating a company's cash generation and management, the cash flow statement can also provide information about a company's liquidity and solvency. By examining the company's cash balance and cash flow from financing activities, investors can determine whether the company has sufficient cash to meet its short-term and long-term financial obligations. This information can be used to evaluate the company's overall financial health and to determine whether it is a good investment opportunity. Here are the main parameters to look for in a cash flow statement analysis:

1. Operating Cash Flow: Operating cash flow measures the amount of cash a company generates from its normal business operations. Analyze trends in operating cash flow to understand a company's ability to generate cash from its core business.

2. Investing Cash Flow: Investing cash flow measures the amount of cash a company spends on investments, such as property, plant, and equipment, and the amount of cash it receives from the sale of investments. Analyze trends in investing cash flow to understand a company's investment strategy and growth potential.

3. Financing Cash Flow: Financing cash flow measures

the amount of cash a company raises or spends on financing activities, such as issuing or repurchasing stock, paying dividends, and taking on or repaying debt. Analyze trends in financing cash flow to understand a company's financial structure and capital raising activities.

4. Free Cash Flow: Free cash flow measures the amount of cash a company generates after subtracting capital expenditures from operating cash flow. Analyze trends in free cash flow to understand a company's ability to fund investments, repay debt, and pay dividends.

5. Cash Balance: The ending cash balance on the cash flow statement provides insights into a company's liquidity and cash position.

6. Cash Conversion Cycle: The cash conversion cycle measures the time it takes for a company to convert inventory into cash. Analyze trends in the cash conversion cycle to understand a company's efficiency in managing its working capital.

7. Capital Expenditures: Capital expenditures are investments in long-term assets such as property, plant, and equipment. Analyze trends in capital expenditures to understand a company's investment strategy and potential for future growth.

When analyzing financial statements, it is important for investors to not only look for positive indicators of a company's financial health but also to be aware of potential red flags that may indicate a risky or potentially poor investment opportunity. Here are some potential red flags to look for in financial statements:

1. Declining Revenue: If a company's revenue is

declining over time, this may be a sign of a weakening market or increasing competition. It is important to investigate why the revenue is declining and whether the company has a plan to address the issue.

2. Negative Cash Flow: Negative cash flow may indicate that a company is not generating enough cash to fund its operations or invest in future growth opportunities. This could be due to poor management or the company's industry experiencing a decline.

3. High Debt-to-Equity Ratio: A high debt-to-equity ratio may indicate that a company has taken on too much debt and is highly leveraged. This can be risky if the company experiences a downturn, as it may struggle to pay off its debts.

4. Overvalued Stock Price: If a company's stock price is significantly higher than its earnings per share or other fundamental metrics, it may be overvalued. This could lead to a correction in the stock price, resulting in losses for investors who bought at the inflated price.

5. Unfavorable Management Practices: Poor management practices, such as a history of legal issues or ethical violations, can indicate a risky investment opportunity. It is important to research the company's management team and their track record before investing.

6. Irregularities in Financial Statements: Financial statements that contain irregularities, such as unexplained changes in accounting methods or discrepancies between reported earnings and cash flow, may indicate potential accounting fraud.

7. Dependence on a Single Customer or Product:

Companies that rely heavily on a single customer or product may be vulnerable to market changes or losing that customer. It is important to investigate the company's diversification strategy and assess the risk of a loss of revenue.

CHAPTER 6.
MARKET TIMING

"Being too far ahead of your time is indistinguishable from being wrong."

Howard Marks

Market timing is an investment strategy that involves attempting to buy and sell securities based on predictions of market movements. Market timing is a complex investment strategy that has been debated in the financial industry for many years.

Pros of Market Timing

1. Potential for higher returns: Market timing has the potential to generate higher returns than a passive investment strategy because it allows investors to take advantage of market trends and movements. By buying low and selling high, investors can maximize their profits.

2. Flexibility: Market timing allows investors to be flexible and adjust their investment strategies according to market conditions. This is especially important during times of economic uncertainty or volatility when traditional investment strategies may not be effective.

3. Risk management: Market timing can be used as a risk management tool by allowing investors to avoid market downturns and minimize losses. By selling securities before a market downturn, investors can reduce their exposure to risk and preserve their capital.

Cons of Market Timing

1. Difficult to predict market movements: The biggest challenge of market timing is predicting market movements accurately. Market timing requires investors to predict market movements based on economic data, news, and other factors that may be difficult to interpret and forecast accurately.

2. Increased transaction costs: Market timing involves frequent buying and selling of securities, which can result in higher transaction costs, including brokerage fees and taxes. These costs can erode the potential returns of a market timing strategy.

3. Emotional biases: Market timing can be influenced by emotional biases, such as fear and greed. These biases can lead investors to make irrational decisions that can result in significant losses.

4. Time and effort: Market timing requires time and effort to analyze market trends and economic data, which can be challenging for individual investors who may not have the resources or expertise to do so effectively.

Howard Marks, a well-known investor, writer, and the co-founder of Oaktree Capital Management, has developed a number of theories about investing and the financial markets, including his thoughts on market timing. He believes that market timing is a difficult and unreliable investment strategy. He argues that attempting to predict short-term market movements is nearly impossible and that investors should instead focus on understanding the underlying value of the assets they are investing in. According to Marks, the key to successful investing is to buy assets when they are undervalued and sell them when they are overvalued, rather than trying to time the market.

One of Marks' central concepts is the idea of "second-level thinking". As per Marks' belief, second-level thinking involves understanding not just the facts and data about a particular investment, but also how other investors are likely to react to that information. Marks believes that successful investing requires investors to think beyond the first-level analysis and consider how other investors are likely to respond to market trends and news. He also emphasizes the importance of risk management in investing. He argues that investors should always be aware of the risks associated with their investments and take steps to manage those risks effectively. This includes being prepared for market downturns and being willing to adjust investment strategies when market conditions change.

Despite his skepticism about market timing, Marks acknowledges that there may be opportunities to take advantage of short-term market movements in some situations. For example, he notes that there may be opportunities to buy assets at a discount during times of market volatility or when investors are panicking. However, Marks believes that these opportunities are rare and that investors should be cautious about trying to time the market.

On the other hand, Michael Burry, a well-known investor, hedge fund manager, and founder of Scion Asset Management, has gained widespread attention for correctly predicting and profiting from the subprime mortgage crisis in 2007-2008. Burry's investment philosophy is centered around value investing and contrarianism, with a particular focus on market timing.

Burry believes that market timing is a crucial component of successful investing. He argues that investors must be patient and willing to wait for the right opportunities to invest. According to Burry, these opportunities often arise when markets are in turmoil or when investors are overly pessimistic about a particular asset class. Burry believes that by taking a contrarian approach and investing when others are selling, investors can achieve significant returns over the long term.

Hiss investment strategy involves careful analysis of individual companies and industries. He believes that investors must focus on understanding the underlying value of the assets they are investing in and must be willing to invest for the long term. Burry often takes large positions in individual stocks or asset classes that he believes are undervalued, even when they are out of favor with other investors.

One of Burry's most famous market timing decisions was his bet against the subprime mortgage market in the mid-2000s. Burry analyzed the underlying value of subprime mortgage bonds and determined that they were overvalued. He then took a large short position in these bonds, betting that they would decline in value. When the subprime mortgage market collapsed in 2007-2008, Burry's bet paid off, and he made significant profits for his investors.

Another example of Burry's successful market timing was his investment in GameStop in early 2021. Burry recognized that GameStop was undervalued and had a significant short interest from other investors. He took a long position in the stock, betting that it would rise in value. When a group of retail investors on Reddit banded together to drive up the price of GameStop and squeeze the short sellers, Burry's bet paid off, and he made a significant profit on his investment.

Investing in stocks can be a daunting prospect for many people, especially those who are new to the world of finance. One of the most important factors to consider when investing in stocks is the time horizon of the investment.

Firstly, the stock market can be volatile in the short term. There are many factors that can cause the market to fluctuate, including changes in interest rates, geopolitical events, and corporate earnings reports. These short-term fluctuations can be difficult to predict and can lead to significant losses for investors who are not prepared. By taking a long-term approach to investing in stocks, investors can weather the ups and downs of the market and avoid making rash decisions based on short-term trends.

Secondly, investing in stocks is all about generating wealth over the long term. The most successful investors are those who are patient and willing to wait for their investments to grow over time. By taking a long-term approach, investors can take advantage of the power of compound interest. As their investments grow, the returns they earn can be reinvested, leading to even greater growth over time. This can result in significant wealth creation over a period of many years.

Thirdly, a long-term approach to investing in stocks can help investors avoid the pitfalls of market timing. Market timing involves trying to predict the short-term movements of the market and buying or selling stocks based on these predictions. This is a risky strategy, as it is difficult to predict the market with any degree of accuracy. Investors who try to time the market often end up buying high and selling low, which can lead to significant losses over time. By taking a long-term approach, investors can avoid the temptation to time the market and instead focus on investing in high-quality companies with strong fundamentals.

Finally, a long-term approach to investing in stocks can help investors stay focused on their goals. It is easy to get caught up in short-term trends and forget about the big picture. By focusing on the long term, investors can stay focused on their goals and avoid making decisions based on emotion or short-term fluctuations in the market.

CHAPTER 7.
MANAGING RISK

"In the short run, the market is a voting machine but in the long run, it is a weighing machine. The more heavily weighed the asset in the market's estimation, the greater the risk that adverse developments will lead to a decline in price."

Benjamin Graham

Stock investing can be a great way to grow your wealth, but it comes with inherent risks. One of the most significant risks associated with stock investing is market risk. Market risk is the risk that the entire market will decline, causing the value of an investor's portfolio to decrease. This type of risk is unpredictable and affects all stocks to some extent, but it is especially relevant for investors who hold a large portion of their portfolio in a single stock or industry.

Market risk is also known as systematic risk, which means that it cannot be eliminated through diversification. This type of risk is caused by macroeconomic factors that affect the entire market, such as changes in interest rates, inflation, or economic growth. For example, a recession or a market crash can cause a significant decline in stock prices, even for companies with strong fundamentals.

The stock market has experienced many crashes throughout history, some of which have had a profound impact on the economy and investors. Here are some of the biggest market crashes in history:

1. The Great Depression (1929): The stock market crash of 1929 is one of the most famous in history. In just four days, the stock market lost 25% of its value, and by 1932, stock prices had fallen by 89%. The crash led to a decade-long economic depression and highlighted the need for better regulation of financial markets.

2. Black Monday (1987): On October 19, 1987, the stock market lost 22.6% of its value, the largest one-day percentage drop in history. The crash was caused by a combination of factors, including computerized trading and an overvaluation of stocks.

3. Dotcom Bubble (2000): The dotcom bubble was a period of rapid growth in internet-related stocks in the late 1990s and early 2000s. The bubble burst in 2000, and many tech companies saw their stock prices plummet. The NASDAQ, which is heavily weighted towards technology stocks, lost 78% of its value from its peak in March 2000 to its low in October 2002.

4. Financial Crisis (2008): The financial crisis of 2008 was caused by a combination of factors, including a housing bubble, risky lending practices, and an over-reliance on debt. The crisis led to a widespread loss of confidence in financial institutions and a global recession. The S&P 500 lost more than half of its value from its peak in October 2007 to its low in March 2009.

5. COVID-19 Pandemic (2020): The COVID-19 pandemic led to a significant market crash in early 2020 as global economies shut down to curb the spread of the

virus. The S&P 500 lost more than 30% of its value in just over a month, although it has since recovered to reach new highs.

These market crashes serve as a reminder of the inherent risks of investing in the stock market. While market crashes can be devastating for investors, they can also provide opportunities for those who are able to weather the storm and invest for the long term. Investors who are exposed to market risk need to be prepared to weather periods of volatility and downturns in the market.

Another way to manage market risk is to have a long-term investment horizon. In the short term, stock prices can be highly volatile and subject to sudden changes. However, over the long term, the stock market tends to grow, and investors who hold onto their investments through market downturns can potentially benefit from future growth.

Investing in the stock market involves taking on various types of risks, including company-specific risks. These risks are specific to individual companies and can have a significant impact on the performance of the company's stock. Here are some of the company-specific risks associated with stock investing:

1. Industry Risk: Some industries are inherently riskier than others. For example, technology companies tend to be more volatile and have higher levels of uncertainty than more established industries like healthcare or utilities. Investing in a company within a high-risk industry can increase the potential for losses.

2. Business Model Risk: A company's business model can also impact its risk profile. For example, companies that rely heavily on a single product or customer are at a higher risk of revenue loss if that product or

customer becomes obsolete or goes out of business.

3. Financial Risk: Financial risk refers to a company's ability to meet its financial obligations. Companies that carry a lot of debt or have weak financials are at a higher risk of defaulting on their debts or going bankrupt. This can lead to significant losses for investors.

4. Management Risk: The performance of a company's management team can also impact its risk profile. Poor management decisions or unethical behavior can lead to financial losses, legal issues, or damage to the company's reputation.

5. Regulatory Risk: Companies are subject to a range of regulations that can impact their operations and financial performance. Changes in regulations can have a significant impact on a company's stock price, particularly if the company is heavily regulated.

It's important for investors to understand these company-specific risks when evaluating potential investments. Conducting thorough research on a company's industry, business model, financials, management team, and regulatory environment can help investors identify and mitigate these risks. Additionally, diversifying investments across multiple companies and industries can help reduce the impact of any single company's risk on an investor's portfolio.

Inflation risk is one of the risks associated with stock investing that investors need to be aware of. Inflation is the general increase in the prices of goods and services over time, and it can have a significant impact on the performance of stocks. Inflation has been a persistent problem throughout history, and there have been several instances of significant inflation crises that have had a profound impact on economies and societies around the world.

Here is some of the biggest inflation crises in history:

1. Germany's Weimar Republic (1921-1924): Following World War I, Germany was forced to pay large reparations to the Allied powers. To finance these payments, the German government began printing money, which led to hyperinflation. By 1923, the value of the German mark had plummeted, and prices were doubling every few days. People were forced to carry wheelbarrows of money just to buy basic necessities, and savings were wiped out overnight.

2. Zimbabwe (2000-2009): In the early 2000s, Zimbabwe's government implemented a land reform program that led to a collapse in agricultural production. This, combined with political instability and government corruption, led to hyperinflation. By 2008, the country's inflation rate had reached an estimated 500 billion percent. People were forced to carry bags of cash just to buy basic goods, and the economy ground to a halt.

3. Venezuela (2016-2020): Venezuela's economy has been in crisis for several years, with hyperinflation being one of the major problems. The country's inflation rate reached an estimated 10 million percent in 2019, and the government has been forced to print more money to finance its spending. This has led to a collapse in the value of the country's currency, widespread shortages of goods, and a mass exodus of people from the country.

4. Hungary (1945-1946): Following World War II, Hungary's economy was in shambles. The government attempted to finance its rebuilding efforts by printing money, which led to hyperinflation. By 1946, prices were doubling every

15 hours, and the country's currency had become virtually worthless. The government was eventually forced to introduce a new currency to stabilize the economy.

5. Brazil (1980s-1990s): In the 1980s and 1990s, Brazil experienced several episodes of high inflation. The country's inflation rate reached a peak of 2,477 percent in 1993. The government implemented several stabilization measures, including introducing a new currency and implementing an inflation-targeting regime, which eventually brought inflation under control.

One of the primary ways that inflation can impact stock performance is through interest rates. As inflation rises, central banks may raise interest rates to help control it. This can lead to higher borrowing costs for companies, which can negatively impact their earnings and cash flow. Additionally, higher interest rates can make bonds and other fixed-income securities more attractive to investors, which can lead to a decrease in demand for stocks and a corresponding drop in stock prices.

Inflation can also impact the purchasing power of a company's earnings. If a company's revenues and profits are not growing at a rate that keeps up with inflation, its earnings may be worth less in real terms over time. This can impact the company's ability to invest in growth opportunities or pay dividends to shareholders.

However, some sectors and industries may be more resilient to inflation than others. For example, companies in the energy and materials sectors may benefit from rising commodity prices as a result of inflation. Similarly, companies with strong pricing power may be able to pass on higher costs to consumers, which can help protect their earnings and stock prices.

Investors can take steps to mitigate inflation risk by including inflation-protected securities, such as Treasury Inflation-Protected Securities (TIPS), in their portfolios. Additionally, investing in sectors and industries that are less sensitive to inflation can also help reduce the impact of inflation on a portfolio.

CHAPTER 8.
MONITORING YOUR PORTFOLIO

"An investment in knowledge pays the best interest."

Benjamin Franklin

To ensure that you are meeting your financial goals and making informed investment decisions, it is essential to track and analyze the performance of your investment portfolio. Therefore, in this chapter, we will explore some effective strategies for monitoring and evaluating the performance of your portfolio:

1. Define your investment goals and risk tolerance: Before tracking your portfolio's performance, you need to define your investment goals and risk tolerance. This will help you to determine the appropriate asset allocation and investment strategy that align with your objectives and risk preferences.

2. Choose a benchmark: A benchmark is a reference point that you can use to compare the performance of your portfolio. It could be an index like the S&P 500 or a similar investment strategy. Choosing a benchmark that closely matches your investment style and objectives is important to make an accurate

comparison.

3. Calculate your returns: Calculate the returns of your portfolio on a regular basis. This can be done manually or by using investment tracking software or an online portfolio tracker. It is important to calculate both absolute returns (the actual return of your portfolio) and relative returns (how your portfolio performed compared to the benchmark).

4. Analyze your portfolio's performance: Once you have calculated your portfolio's returns, analyze the performance to identify the strengths and weaknesses of your investments. Look at the individual performance of each holding, the asset allocation, and the overall portfolio diversification. Evaluate if your portfolio is meeting your investment goals and if there are any changes that need to be made.

5. Rebalance your portfolio: Rebalancing your portfolio is important to maintain your desired asset allocation and manage risk. This involves selling holdings that have performed well and buying more of the underperforming assets. Rebalancing should be done on a regular basis to ensure that your portfolio stays aligned with your investment goals.

6. Keep track of expenses: Keeping track of the expenses associated with your portfolio is important to evaluate the impact on your returns. High expenses can erode your returns, so it is important to evaluate if the expenses are worth the cost.

When it comes to analyzing stocks, understanding and analyzing key performance indicators (KPIs) is essential to making informed investment decisions. KPIs are financial metrics that are used to measure the performance of a company and its stock. Some of the most commonly used KPIs in stock analysis include revenue growth, earnings per share (EPS), price-to-earnings ratio (P/E ratio), return on equity (ROE), and dividend yield:

1. Revenue Growth: Revenue growth is a measure of how much a company's revenue has increased over a given period of time, typically on an annual basis. A high revenue growth rate is generally seen as a positive sign for a company, as it indicates that the company is growing and generating more revenue. Investors should compare a company's revenue growth rate to that of its competitors and industry benchmarks to gauge its relative performance.

2. Earnings Per Share (EPS): EPS is a measure of a company's profitability that represents the amount of earnings per share of stock. A high EPS is generally seen as a positive sign for a company, as it indicates that it is generating more profit per share of stock. Investors should compare a company's EPS to that of its competitors and historical data to gauge its relative performance.

3. Price-to-Earnings Ratio (P/E Ratio): The P/E ratio is the ratio of a company's share price to its EPS. It is used to determine if a stock is overvalued or undervalued. A high P/E ratio suggests that a stock may be overvalued, while a low P/E ratio suggests that it may be undervalued. Investors should compare a company's P/E ratio to that of its competitors and historical data to gauge its relative performance.

4. Return on Equity (ROE): ROE measures a company's profitability by comparing its net income to its shareholders' equity. A high ROE is generally seen as a positive sign for a company, as it indicates that it is

generating more profit for its shareholders. Investors should compare a company's ROE to that of its competitors and historical data to gauge its relative performance.

5. Dividend Yield: Dividend yield measures the annual dividend payment divided by the stock price. It is used to determine the return on investment from a stock's dividend payments. A high dividend yield is generally seen as a positive sign for a company, as it indicates that it is returning value to its shareholders. Investors should compare a company's dividend yield to that of its competitors and historical data to gauge its relative performance.

To effectively analyze KPIs of a stock, it's important to track them over time and compare them to industry benchmarks and historical data. This can help identify trends and potential areas of improvement or concern. Additionally, it's important to consider any external factors that may be affecting the KPIs, such as changes in the market, new competitors, or regulatory changes.

Technical analysis is a method of evaluating securities based on statistics generated by market activity, such as past prices and volume. Technical analysts use charts and other tools to identify patterns and trends that can help them make informed investment decisions. Here are some key steps to interpreting technical analysis charts.

1. Choose a Chart Type: There are several types of charts that can be used for technical analysis, including line charts, bar charts, and candlestick charts. Line charts show a single line representing the price over a specified period, while bar charts show a series of vertical bars representing the price range for each day or week. Candlestick charts are similar to bar charts,

but use colored boxes and lines to show the price range for each period.

2. Identify Trendlines: Trendlines are lines drawn on a chart that connect two or more points on the chart, representing a trend in the direction of the line. An upward sloping trendline represents an uptrend, while a downward sloping trendline represents a downtrend.

3. Use Indicators: Indicators are tools that can be added to a chart to help identify trends and potential buy or sell signals. Some commonly used indicators include moving averages, relative strength index (RSI), and MACD (moving average convergence divergence). Moving averages can help identify the direction of the trend, while RSI can help identify overbought or oversold conditions. MACD can help identify changes in trend direction.

4. Analyze Chart Patterns: Chart patterns are formations on a chart that can provide clues about potential trend reversals or continuations. Some commonly used chart patterns include head and shoulders, triangles, and flags. Head and shoulders patterns can signal a potential reversal of an uptrend, while triangles and flags can indicate a continuation of the current trend.

5. Consider Volume: Volume is the total number of shares or contracts traded during a specified period. Increasing volume can be a sign of strong buying or selling pressure, while decreasing volume can indicate a lack of interest in the security.

6. Monitor Support and Resistance Levels: Support and resistance levels are price levels where the stock has previously struggled to move above or below.

These levels can indicate potential buying or selling opportunities, as well as potential areas of price reversal.

Overall, interpreting technical analysis charts requires a combination of knowledge, experience, and attention to detail. By understanding the different chart types, trendlines, indicators, chart patterns, volume, and support and resistance levels, investors can better assess the potential direction of a security and make informed investment decisions.

CHAPTER 9. COMMON MISTAKES TO AVOID

"The financial markets generally are unpredictable. So that one has to have different scenarios. The idea that you can actually predict what's going to happen contradicts my way of looking at the market."

George Soros

Many people turn to the stock market as a way to grow their wealth over time. However, investing in stocks can be risky and unpredictable. Even seasoned investors can make mistakes that lead to significant financial losses. Let's discuss some of the most common mistakes people make when investing in stocks and how to avoid them.

1. Lack of research: One of the biggest mistakes investors make is not doing enough research before investing. For example, investing in a company without understanding its business model, competitive landscape, and financial performance can be risky. To avoid this mistake, take the time to research the company's fundamentals and assess its long-term prospects.

2. Emotional investing: Emotions can drive investors to make impulsive decisions that lead to significant losses. Fear and greed, in particular, can cloud your judgment and cause you to buy or sell stocks at

the wrong time. To avoid this mistake, create a well-thought-out investment plan and stick to it, regardless of short-term market fluctuations.

3. Trying to time the market: Trying to buy stocks at the lowest possible price and sell them at the highest possible price is nearly impossible to do consistently. Instead, focus on long-term investing and invest in a diversified portfolio of stocks that aligns with your investment goals.

4. Not diversifying: Investing all your money in one stock or sector can be risky. If that company or sector experiences a downturn, you could lose a significant portion of your investment. To avoid this mistake, diversify your portfolio by investing in different sectors, asset classes, and geographies.

5. Not having a long-term plan: Investing in stocks without a long-term plan can lead to short-term thinking and impulsive decisions. To avoid this mistake, create a well-defined investment plan that aligns with your goals, and stick to it, regardless of short-term market fluctuations.

6. Overconfidence: Overconfidence can lead investors to take unnecessary risks and believe they can consistently outperform the market. To avoid this mistake, remain humble and objective and stick to a well-thought-out investment strategy.

7. Not considering fees: Fees associated with investing in stocks, such as brokerage fees, transaction fees, and management fees, can eat into your returns over time. To avoid this mistake, understand the fees associated with investing in stocks and factor them into your investment strategy.

In 2016, a healthcare startup called Theranos was valued at a whopping $9 billion. The company's founder, Elizabeth Holmes, was hailed as a visionary and potential game-changer in the healthcare industry. Theranos aimed to revolutionize the blood testing industry by developing a technology that could run multiple tests on a single drop of blood. However, it was later revealed that the technology was faulty, and Holmes was indicted for fraud. Many investors who had put their money into the company without doing proper research lost a significant amount of money. The Theranos case serves as a cautionary tale of the risks of blindly investing in a company without thoroughly investigating its technology, management, and financials.

The case also raised questions about the role of Silicon Valley and the culture of startups in promoting and perpetuating fraudulent behavior. Theranos received significant investment and praise from prominent figures in the technology industry, and many overlooked red flags about the company's technology and capabilities. This has led to a larger conversation about the need for greater scrutiny and regulation in the healthcare industry, particularly in the context of startups and emerging technologies.

One of the most significant stock investment mistakes in recent years has been the case of WeWork, a company that offers shared workspace solutions to businesses of all sizes. In early 2019, WeWork was valued at a staggering $47 billion, making it one of the most valuable startups in the world. However, by the end of the year, the company's value had plummeted to less than $8 billion, and its planned initial public offering (IPO) was canceled.

The WeWork saga is a classic example of a company that was overhyped and overvalued by investors who failed to look closely at its business model and financials. WeWork's valuation was largely based on its ability to disrupt the traditional office leasing market and capitalize on the growing trend of remote work. However, the company's financials were questionable, with losses mounting each year and no clear path to profitability.

One of the primary reasons for WeWork's downfall was the leadership of its founder, Adam Neumann. Neumann was known for his extravagant lifestyle, which included owning multiple homes, private jets, and a personal surf instructor. He also had a controversial management style, which included making impulsive decisions and disregarding feedback from his advisors and board members.

CHAPTER 10.
INVESTING IN
EXCHANGE-TRADED
FUNDS (ETFS)

"I am a big fan of the ETF. It's the best thing to happen to the individual investor in the last twenty years."

Burton Malkiel

Exchange-Traded Funds (ETFs) are investment vehicles that are growing in popularity among individual investors due to their flexibility and lower fees compared to traditional mutual funds. ETFs are similar to mutual funds in that they hold a portfolio of securities, such as stocks or bonds, but they are traded on exchanges like stocks. If you're interested in investing in ETFs, here are some basic steps to get started:

1. Determine your investment objectives and risk tolerance: Before investing in any ETF, you need to determine your investment goals, risk tolerance, and time horizon. If you are investing for the long term, such as retirement, you may want to consider investing in a diversified portfolio of ETFs that include both stocks and bonds. If you are investing for

the short term, such as saving for a down payment on a house, you may want to consider a low-risk ETF that invests in high-quality bonds.

2. Choose the right ETF: There are thousands of ETFs available, and each has a different investment strategy. Some ETFs track a specific index, such as the S&P 500, while others invest in specific sectors, such as technology or healthcare. You should choose an ETF that aligns with your investment goals and risk tolerance.

3. Research the ETF: Before investing in an ETF, you should research the ETF's performance, fees, and holdings. You can find this information on the ETF provider's website or through financial news outlets. You should also read the ETF's prospectus, which provides detailed information about the ETF's investment strategy, risks, and fees.

4. Open an investment account: To invest in an ETF, you need to open an investment account with a brokerage firm. Most brokerage firms offer commission-free trading of ETFs. You should compare brokerage firms to find one that offers low fees and meets your investment needs.

5. Place a trade: Once you have chosen an ETF and opened an investment account, you can place a trade to buy the ETF. You can place a trade through your brokerage firm's website or mobile app. When placing a trade, you should enter the ticker symbol of the ETF, the number of shares you want to buy, and the price you are willing to pay.

6. Monitor your investment: After you have invested in an ETF, you should monitor your investment regularly to ensure it aligns with your investment

goals and risk tolerance. You should also rebalance your portfolio periodically to ensure you maintain your desired asset allocation.

For investors, the importance of investing in ETFs with lower fees cannot be overstated, as it can have a significant impact on their investment returns over the long term. Firstly, lower fees mean more money in your pocket. Fees, also known as expense ratios, are the ongoing costs that investors pay to own an ETF. These fees are deducted from the ETF's net asset value (NAV) and can have a significant impact on investment returns over the long term. For example, if an ETF has an expense ratio of 0.5%, and an investor has a $10,000 investment in the ETF, they would pay $50 in fees annually. Over the course of ten years, this would add up to $500 in fees, which can have a significant impact on investment returns. By investing in ETFs with lower fees, investors can reduce their costs and keep more of their investment returns.

Secondly, lower fees can lead to higher investment returns. Fees can eat into investment returns over the long term, as they reduce the amount of money that is available to compound over time. Compound interest is a powerful tool for investors, as it allows them to earn interest on their principal investment and any interest or dividends that are reinvested over time. By reducing the amount of money that is deducted from the NAV of an ETF, investors can keep more of their investment returns and benefit from the power of compounding.

Thirdly, lower fees can help investors achieve their financial goals. Investing in ETFs with lower fees can help investors achieve their financial goals by reducing their costs and increasing their investment returns. For example, if an investor is saving for retirement, reducing their investment costs can help them save more money over time and potentially retire earlier. Here are some ETFs with the lowest fees that are suitable for someone who is new to investing:

1. Vanguard Total Stock Market ETF (VTI): This ETF tracks the performance of the CRSP US Total Market Index, which includes small-, mid-, and large-cap US stocks. With an expense ratio of only 0.03%, VTI is one of the cheapest ETFs on the market. This ETF offers broad exposure to the US stock market and has consistently outperformed its benchmark over the long term.

2. iShares Core S&P 500 ETF (IVV): This ETF tracks the performance of the S&P 500, which is a widely followed index of large-cap US stocks. With an expense ratio of 0.03%, IVV is another low-cost option for investors seeking exposure to the US stock market. This ETF is a great option for those who want exposure to some of the biggest and most well-known companies in the US.

3. Schwab US Broad Market ETF (SCHB): This ETF tracks the performance of the Dow Jones US Broad Stock Market Index, which includes small-, mid-, and large-cap US stocks. With an expense ratio of only 0.03%, SCHB is one of the cheapest ETFs on the market. This ETF offers broad exposure to the US stock market and has a good track record of performance.

4. Vanguard Total Bond Market ETF (BND): This ETF tracks the performance of the Bloomberg Barclays US Aggregate Bond Index, which includes investment-grade US bonds. With an expense ratio of 0.04%, BND is one of the cheapest bond ETFs available. This ETF is a great option for investors seeking exposure to the US bond market and can be a valuable diversification tool for those who also hold equity ETFs.

5. iShares Core MSCI EAFE ETF (IEFA): This ETF tracks the performance of the MSCI EAFE Index, which

includes stocks from developed markets outside of the US and Canada. With an expense ratio of 0.07%, IEFA is a low-cost way to gain exposure to international equity markets. This ETF is a great option for those who want to diversify their portfolio beyond the US stock market.

CHAPTER 11. GLOBAL STOCK MARKET

"Investing should be more like watching paint dry or watching grass grow. If you want excitement, take $800 and go to Las Vegas."

Paul Samuelson

The global stock market is a vast and complex system that can be challenging to navigate for even the most seasoned investors. It is made up of thousands of companies from around the world, each with its unique characteristics, risks, and potential rewards.

Some of these companies are large multinational corporations with operations in multiple countries and regions, while others are smaller, more specialized companies focused on a specific niche or market segment. Investing in the global stock market can offer tremendous opportunities for wealth creation over the long term, but it requires the right knowledge and strategy to navigate the risks and capitalize on the rewards.

The world is home to many different stock markets, each with its unique characteristics, opportunities, and risks. Here's an overview of some of the major stock markets in the world:

1. New York Stock Exchange (NYSE): The NYSE is the largest and most well-known stock exchange in the world, with over 2,800 listed companies and a market capitalization of over $30 trillion. It's home to some

of the world's largest and most iconic companies, including Apple, Microsoft, and Coca-Cola.

2. NASDAQ: The NASDAQ is a global electronic marketplace for buying and selling securities, and it's the second-largest stock exchange in the world by market capitalization. It's home to many technology companies such as Amazon, Facebook, and Google.

3. Tokyo Stock Exchange (TSE): The TSE is the third-largest stock exchange in the world by market capitalization and the largest in Asia. It's home to some of Japan's most prominent companies, such as Toyota, Mitsubishi, and Sony.

4. Shanghai Stock Exchange (SSE): The SSE is one of the largest stock exchanges in the world, with a market capitalization of over $4 trillion. It's the main stock exchange in mainland China, and it's home to many of China's largest companies, such as Alibaba, China Mobile, and PetroChina.

5. Hong Kong Stock Exchange (HKEX): The HKEX is the main stock exchange in Hong Kong, and it's one of the largest stock exchanges in Asia. It's home to many of China's largest companies, as well as international companies such as HSBC, Tencent, and Alibaba.

6. London Stock Exchange (LSE): The LSE is one of the oldest and most established stock exchanges in the world, with a market capitalization of over $4 trillion. It's home to some of the UK's largest and most well-known companies, such as BP, Royal Dutch Shell, and GlaxoSmithKline.

7. Euronext: The Euronext is a pan-European stock exchange that operates in Amsterdam, Brussels, Dublin, Lisbon, Oslo, and Paris. It's the largest stock

exchange in Europe, with a market capitalization of over $5 trillion.

One of the benefits of investing in the global stock market is that it allows investors to build diversified portfolios that can potentially offer higher returns and lower risk than investing in a single country or region. By investing in a range of companies from different countries and industries, investors can spread their risk and potentially benefit from the growth opportunities offered by the global economy.

However, investing in the global stock market also requires a solid understanding of the risks involved. Political and economic instability, regulatory changes, and currency fluctuations can all impact the performance of companies and markets around the world. It's important for investors to carefully evaluate the risks associated with different companies and regions and to build a portfolio that reflects their risk tolerance and investment objectives.

One of the keys to successful investing in the global stock market is to focus on companies with strong fundamentals and competitive advantages. Companies with solid financials, a strong market position, and a proven track record of performance are more likely to weather market downturns and continue to grow over the long term.

Another important factor to consider when investing in the global stock market is the role of technology and innovation. Many of the most successful companies in the global stock market are those that are at the forefront of technological innovation, from e-commerce giants like Amazon to software companies like Microsoft.

The global economy is home to many large multinational corporations that have a significant presence in countries around the world. Here's an overview of some of the major listed companies with a worldwide presence:

1. Apple Inc.: A technology giant and one of the most valuable companies in the world. Its products, such as the iPhone, iPad, and Mac computers, are sold in countries around the world. It has operations in Asia, Europe, North and South America, and Australia.

2. ExxonMobil: One of the largest oil and gas companies in the world, with operations in over 200 countries. Its primary business is the exploration, production, and distribution of oil, gas, and petroleum products. Its operations span the Americas, Europe, Asia Pacific, the Middle East, and Africa.

3. Toyota: One of the world's largest car manufacturers, with a presence in over 170 countries. It has manufacturing plants and sales offices across the Americas, Europe, Asia Pacific, the Middle East, and Africa. Toyota is known for producing reliable and efficient vehicles, such as the Corolla, Camry, and Prius.

4. Coca-Cola: A beverage giant that operates in over 200 countries. It's known for its iconic soft drink, Coca-Cola, as well as other popular brands such as Sprite, Fanta, and Dasani. Coca-Cola has a significant presence in North and South America, Europe, Asia Pacific, and Africa.

5. Samsung Electronics: A South Korean multinational conglomerate that operates in various industries, such as electronics, semiconductors, and telecommunications. Its products, such as smartphones, TVs, and home appliances, are sold in countries around the world. Samsung has a significant presence in Asia, Europe, North and South America, and Africa.

6. Amazon: One of the largest e-commerce companies in the world, with operations in North America, Europe, Asia Pacific, and the Middle East. Its online marketplace sells a vast array of products, from books to electronics to clothing. Amazon has also expanded into other businesses, such as cloud computing and entertainment.

7. Nestle: A Swiss multinational food and beverage company that operates in over 190 countries. Its brands, such as KitKat, Nescafe, and Purina, are sold worldwide. Nestle is known for its focus on sustainability and has set ambitious targets for reducing its environmental impact.

As the global economy continues to expand, many companies are experiencing rapid growth and expanding their reach into new markets. Listed companies, in particular, are often in the spotlight as they provide investors with an opportunity to participate in their growth. Here are some of the fastest-growing listed companies with a significant presence worldwide:

1. Zoom Video Communications Inc.: A video conferencing software company that experienced a surge in demand during the COVID-19 pandemic. With more people working and studying from home, the need for remote communication tools has grown exponentially. As a result, Zoom's revenue increased by 355% in 2020, and the company's stock price surged by over 500% in the same year. Zoom's software is now used by millions of people worldwide and has become an essential tool for businesses, schools, and organizations around the world.

2. Tesla Inc.: An electric vehicle (EV) manufacturer that has seen tremendous growth in recent years. The

company has disrupted the traditional automotive industry and has quickly become one of the most valuable carmakers in the world. Tesla's revenue grew by 68% in 2020, and its market capitalization exceeded that of traditional automakers such as Ford and General Motors. Tesla's global presence continues to expand, with the company opening new factories and introducing new models in markets around the world.

3. Alibaba Group Holding Ltd.: A Chinese e-commerce giant that has rapidly grown to become one of the largest companies in the world. The company's revenue increased by 41% in 2020, driven by a surge in online shopping during the pandemic. Alibaba's presence extends beyond China, with the company expanding into new markets such as Southeast Asia and Europe. With a market capitalization of over $500 billion, Alibaba is one of the most valuable companies in the world and continues to experience rapid growth.

4. MercadoLibre Inc.: A Latin American e-commerce and fintech company that has been growing rapidly in recent years. The company's revenue grew by 73% in 2020, driven by a surge in online shopping in the region. MercadoLibre operates in 18 countries in Latin America and has over 76 million active users. The company's fintech division, MercadoPago, is also experiencing rapid growth, with the company expanding into new markets and introducing new services such as digital payments and credit.

5. Sea Ltd.: A Singapore-based company that operates in three main areas: e-commerce, gaming, and digital payments. The company's revenue grew by 101% in 2020, driven by strong growth in its gaming

and e-commerce divisions. Sea operates primarily in Southeast Asia but has recently expanded into new markets such as Latin America. With a market capitalization of over $100 billion, Sea is one of the most valuable companies in Southeast Asia and is continuing to experience rapid growth.

These are just a few examples of the fastest-growing listed companies with a significant global presence. While past performance does not guarantee future success, these companies have shown a remarkable ability to adapt to changing market conditions and capture new opportunities for growth. As such, they may be worth considering for investors seeking exposure to high-growth companies with a global reach.

Investing in dividend aristocrats can be a good strategy for income-seeking investors because these companies have a proven track record of increasing their dividends over the long term. Dividend aristocrats are companies that have consistently increased their dividend payments to shareholders for at least 25 consecutive years. These companies are known for their stability and reliability, and they are often viewed as good long-term investments because of their consistent dividend payments. Some examples of global companies that are considered dividend aristocrats include:

1. Procter & Gamble Co. (NYSE: PG): Procter & Gamble is a consumer goods company that produces a wide range of products, including cleaning supplies, personal care items, and baby products. The company operates in over 180 countries and has a diverse portfolio of brands, including Tide, Pampers, and Gillette. Procter & Gamble has increased its dividend for over 60 consecutive years, making it one of the most reliable dividend-paying companies in the world.

2. Johnson & Johnson (NYSE: JNJ): This healthcare company is known for producing medical devices, pharmaceuticals, and consumer healthcare products. Johnson & Johnson has a global presence, with operations in over 60 countries. The company has increased its dividend for over 50 consecutive years and is viewed as a stable, long-term investment.

3. PepsiCo Inc. (PEP): This food and beverage giant has increased its dividend for 49 consecutive years and has a current yield of around 2.8%. The company's portfolio of brands includes Pepsi, Frito-Lay, Quaker Oats, and Tropicana, among others.

4. Colgate-Palmolive Co. (CL): This consumer goods company has increased its dividend for 58 consecutive years and has a current yield of around 2.2%. The company's products, which include toothpaste, soap, and other household items, are sold in over 200 countries worldwide.

However, it's important to note that past performance is not indicative of future results, and thorough research and analysis should be conducted before making any investment decisions. Additionally, while dividend aristocrats are known for their stability, they may not always offer the same level of growth potential as other, more volatile investments.

CHAPTER 12. UNDERSTANDING MACRO AND MICROECONOMIC FACTORS

"Markets and economies are driven by people's reactions to information, not by the information itself."

Ray Dalio

Macro and microeconomics are two different branches of economics that focus on different aspects of the economy, but they are closely related and often influence each other. Macroeconomics deals with the overall performance and behavior of the economy, while microeconomics focuses on the behavior of individual consumers, firms, and markets.

Macroeconomics is the study of the overall performance and behavior of the economy as a whole. It deals with issues such as economic growth, inflation, unemployment, and international trade. Understanding macroeconomic factors is essential for investors, policymakers, and anyone interested in the health and stability of the economy.

One of the most important macroeconomic factors is gross domestic product (GDP). GDP measures the total value of goods and services produced in a country over a given period of time, typically a year. It is an important indicator of economic growth, as higher GDP generally indicates a stronger and more prosperous economy. However, it's important to note that GDP alone does not provide a complete picture of the economy's health. For example, GDP may be high but the benefits may not be evenly distributed across the population.

Another key macroeconomic factor is inflation, which measures the rate at which prices of goods and services are rising. Inflation can have a significant impact on the economy, as it can erode the purchasing power of consumers and reduce the value of investments. Central banks and policymakers closely monitor inflation and may take measures to control it, such as adjusting interest rates or implementing monetary policies.

Unemployment is another important macroeconomic factor. High unemployment rates can be a sign of a weak economy, as it indicates a lack of job opportunities and reduced consumer spending. Unemployment occurs when individuals who are willing and able to work cannot find employment. High levels of unemployment can have a significant impact on the economy, as it leads to lower consumer spending, reduced production, and decreased economic growth.

When unemployment is high, people have less money to spend, and businesses have less demand for their products or services. This can lead to a downward spiral, with reduced production leading to layoffs and higher unemployment, which, in turn, leads to even lower consumer spending and economic growth.

One of the most significant unemployment rates in history was during the Great Depression, which lasted from 1929 to 1939. At its peak in 1933, the unemployment rate in the United States was 24.9%. The Great Depression was triggered by the stock market crash of 1929 and led to a significant decrease in GDP, rising unemployment, and a decline in the standard of living for many Americans.

In the 1970s, there was another significant period of high unemployment, known as the Stagflation period. Stagflation is a combination of high inflation and high unemployment, which is a unique phenomenon as the two typically have an inverse relationship. During the Stagflation period, which lasted from 1973 to 1982, the unemployment rate in the United States peaked at 9.7% in 1982.

In more recent times, the global financial crisis of 2008 led to a significant increase in unemployment rates around the world. In the United States, the unemployment rate peaked at 10% in October 2009, while in the European Union, the unemployment rate reached a high of 10.9% in 2013.

The COVID-19 pandemic of 2020 also had a significant impact on unemployment rates globally. With widespread business closures and job losses, the global unemployment rate rose from 5.4% in 2019 to 6% in 2020. While some countries have shown signs of recovery, the pandemic's impact on the global economy is still significant.

On the other hand, low unemployment rates can lead to wage growth and increased consumer spending, which can stimulate economic growth. Policymakers often implement measures to reduce unemployment, such as job training programs or tax incentives for businesses that create new jobs.

International trade is also a significant macroeconomic factor. The balance of trade, or the difference between a country's imports and exports, can have a significant impact on the economy. A trade deficit, where a country imports more than it exports, can lead to a decrease in GDP and a weakened economy. On the other hand, a trade surplus, where a country exports more than it imports, can lead to increased economic growth and stability.

Government policies and fiscal measures can have a significant impact on the economy as a whole. Tax policies, government spending, and monetary policies all influence macroeconomic factors such as GDP, inflation, and unemployment. Understanding the impact of these policies is important for investors and policymakers alike, as they can have far-reaching effects on the economy and the financial markets.

Microeconomics is a branch of economics that deals with the study of individual decision-making units such as consumers, households, and firms. Microeconomic factors, therefore, refer to the economic factors that affect the decision-making behavior of these units. One of the most important microeconomic factors is price. Price plays a critical role in the decision-making process of both consumers and firms. Consumers are always looking for the best value for their money, while firms are always trying to maximize profits. Prices influence consumer behavior by affecting their purchasing power and their perception of the value of goods and services. For firms, prices determine the amount of revenue they can generate and ultimately affect their profitability.

Another microeconomic factor is competition. Competition is a driving force in the market economy and influences the behavior of both consumers and firms. Consumers have more options to choose from when there is competition, which in turn puts pressure on firms to improve the quality of their products and services while keeping prices competitive. Firms, on the other hand, are constantly seeking to gain an advantage over their competitors by improving their products, offering better customer service, and lowering prices.

The third microeconomic factor is income. Income is a critical factor that influences the purchasing power of consumers. Consumers with higher incomes have more disposable income and can afford to purchase more goods and services. Firms also pay close attention to income levels when setting prices and designing marketing strategies. High-income consumers are often targeted for luxury products and services, while low-income consumers may be targeted for value-based products and services.

The fourth microeconomic factor is consumer preferences. Consumer preferences refer to the specific needs and wants of consumers. These preferences can be influenced by a variety of factors, including age, gender, income level, and cultural background. Firms must pay close attention to consumer preferences when designing products and services and developing marketing strategies. By understanding consumer preferences, firms can tailor their offerings to better meet the needs of their target market. In today's globalized and highly competitive marketplace, achieving a dominant market position is a significant achievement for any company. Companies with high market share are typically able to maintain strong profits, generate cash flow, and drive growth through economies of scale.

One such company is Amazon, which is currently the largest e-commerce retailer in the world. Amazon's success can be attributed to its aggressive expansion strategy, which has led to a significant increase in the company's market share over the past few years. The company has expanded its offerings beyond books and is now a major player in many other product categories such as electronics, fashion, and home goods. Amazon's continued focus on improving its customer experience through a wide range of products, competitive pricing, and fast delivery has also contributed to its success.

Google is another example of a worldwide listed company with great market share in its field. As the world's leading search engine, Google has become an essential tool for users around the world. Google's success can be attributed to its powerful search algorithms, which are able to provide users with highly relevant search results. The company's focus on user experience has also played a key role in its success, with the company investing heavily in improving its user interface and providing users with a seamless search experience. Google's acquisition of other companies such as YouTube and Android has also contributed to its market dominance in the technology industry.

The fifth microeconomic factor is technology. Technological advancements have revolutionized the way businesses operate and interact with consumers. New technologies have made it easier and more cost-effective for firms to produce and distribute goods and services. They have also created new markets and new opportunities for firms to reach customers. Firms must be aware of technological advancements and adapt their operations to remain competitive in the market.

Over the years, several publicly traded companies have achieved significant technological advancements that have helped to catapult their stock value. These companies have been able to generate significant returns for their shareholders by investing in research and development and staying ahead of their competitors. One of the most well-known companies in this regard is Apple Inc. (AAPL). Founded in 1976 by Steve Jobs, Steve Wozniak, and Ronald Wayne, the company started out as a manufacturer of personal computers. However, over the years, it has grown to become one of the most valuable companies in the world, with a market capitalization of over $2 trillion as of 2021. One of the key factors that has helped Apple to achieve this success is its ability to innovate.

Apple's innovation can be traced back to its early days when it introduced the Macintosh personal computer, which featured a graphical user interface and a mouse, making it easier for users to interact with their computers. This innovation helped to set Apple apart from its competitors and establish it as a leader in the personal computer industry. Since then, Apple has continued to innovate, introducing the iPod, iPhone, and iPad, each of which has been a game-changer in its respective market.

Another company that has achieved significant technological advancements is Tesla, Inc. (TSLA). Founded in 2003 by Elon Musk, Tesla is a company that is focused on creating sustainable transportation solutions. The company has developed a range of electric vehicles that are powered by advanced battery technology. One of the key factors that has helped Tesla to achieve its success is its ability to innovate in the electric vehicle space.

One of the most significant technological advancements that Tesla has made is the development of its Autopilot technology. This technology allows Tesla vehicles to operate autonomously, with the car's computer controlling the steering, acceleration, and braking. While the technology is not yet fully autonomous, it has helped to establish Tesla as a leader in the electric vehicle market and has helped to drive its stock price higher.

CHAPTER 13. THE PSYCHOLOGY OF INVESTING AND MANAGING EMOTIONS

"Cultivate the calmness of a king or queen in the face of chaos, and you'll find that you can navigate through anything. This is especially true when it comes to investing, where managing your emotions is just as important as managing your money."

Tony Robbins.

The psychology of investing is a complex subject, and it encompasses several aspects. One of the critical elements of investing is risk management. Every investment carries a certain degree of risk, and the degree of risk varies depending on the type of investment. Stocks, for instance, are generally riskier than bonds or real estate. Understanding the risk associated with an investment is crucial to making informed investment decisions. However, managing risk is not just a matter of analyzing data. Emotions play a significant role in risk management. Fear and greed are two of the most powerful emotions that can influence investment decisions. Fear can lead to a reluctance to invest, even in relatively safe investments, while greed can lead to excessive risk-taking, leading to significant losses.

Tulip Mania was one of the most famous financial bubbles in history, occurring in the Netherlands in the 17th century. The event involved the speculative trading of tulip bulbs, which reached an unprecedented level of value before ultimately crashing, causing significant financial losses for investors. Tulip Mania serves as a cautionary tale about the dangers of speculation and the irrational exuberance that can drive market bubbles.

In the early 17th century, the Netherlands experienced an economic boom, driven in part by an increase in trade and commerce. During this time, tulips were a highly sought-after commodity, prized for their exotic beauty and rarity. As demand for tulips grew, so did their price, with some bulbs selling for exorbitant sums of money. As tulip fever gripped the country, investors began to speculate on the price of tulips, buying and selling bulbs for ever-increasing sums.

At the height of Tulip Mania, tulip bulbs became so valuable that they were used as a form of currency. People mortgaged their homes and sold their possessions to purchase bulbs in hopes of making a quick profit. Some investors became incredibly wealthy, while others lost everything.

The tulip market was based on a futures contract system, where investors could purchase the right to buy a specific bulb at a future date for a set price. As the price of tulips skyrocketed, futures contracts became increasingly popular, with some bulbs being sold multiple times before they had even been dug up from the ground.

In 1637, the tulip market abruptly crashed, with prices plummeting nearly overnight. Investors who had mortgaged their homes and invested all of their savings into tulips were left with nothing. The Dutch government attempted to intervene, but it was too late to prevent significant financial losses.

Tulip Mania had a lasting impact on the Dutch economy, leading to widespread financial hardship and the collapse of many businesses. It also served as a warning about the dangers of speculation and the irrational exuberance that can drive market bubbles.

In hindsight, the tulip market was a classic example of a speculative bubble, fueled by the belief that tulips would continue to rise in value indefinitely. The market was driven by greed and speculation, rather than any fundamental value or underlying economic reality. As such, it serves as a reminder that market bubbles can arise in any asset class, and investors should exercise caution and avoid being swept up in the hype of a speculative frenzy.

Another aspect of the psychology of investing is the role of biases. Bias refers to a tendency to favor a particular point of view or perspective. Many cognitive biases can affect investment decisions. Confirmation bias, for example, refers to the tendency to seek out information that confirms pre-existing beliefs or hypotheses. This bias can lead investors to ignore critical information that contradicts their preconceived notions about an investment. Other biases, such as the availability heuristic, refer to the tendency to overestimate the likelihood of events based on the ease with which they come to mind. This bias can lead investors to overestimate the potential returns of an investment based on recent news or events.

One notable example of confirmation bias in action was the collapse of Enron, a US energy company that was involved in one of the largest corporate scandals in history. In the early 2000s, Enron was widely regarded as a high-performing company, with a stock price that had increased rapidly over several years. However, this growth was based on fraudulent accounting practices and misleading financial statements, which were used to conceal massive losses.

Despite warning signs that Enron was engaged in unethical and illegal activities, many investors continued to hold onto their

Enron stock and even purchased additional shares. This was in part due to confirmation bias, as investors sought out information that supported their belief that Enron was a strong investment opportunity, while ignoring information that contradicted this belief.

The collapse of Enron serves as a cautionary tale about the dangers of confirmation bias in the stock market. It highlights the importance of conducting thorough research and considering multiple sources of information when making investment decisions. Investors must be willing to challenge their own assumptions and seek out information that contradicts their beliefs in order to make informed and rational investment decisions.

The psychology of investing also involves understanding the role of emotions in decision-making. Emotions such as fear, greed, and hope can influence investment decisions. Fear can cause investors to sell their investments prematurely, while greed can lead to overconfidence and a willingness to take on too much risk. Hope can lead investors to hold onto poorly performing investments, hoping for a turnaround. Understanding the role of emotions in investment decisions is crucial to making informed decisions.

One of the most significant events related to a stock that was driven by fear was the market crash of 1987, also known as Black Monday. On October 19, 1987, the stock market experienced a sudden and severe decline, with the Dow Jones Industrial Average falling by more than 22% in a single day. This decline was driven by a combination of factors, including rising interest rates, concerns about trade imbalances, and a growing sense of fear and panic among investors.

Leading up to the market crash, there were several warning signs that suggested the market was overvalued and at risk of a sudden decline. For example, the price-to-earnings ratios of many stocks were at historically high levels, and there were growing concerns about corporate debt levels and inflation. Despite these warning signs, many investors remained bullish and continued to pour money into the market, fueling a speculative bubble.

On the morning of October 19, 1987, the stock market opened with a sharp decline, triggering a wave of panic selling among investors. As the market continued to decline throughout the day, fear and uncertainty spread, with many investors rushing to sell their stocks in order to avoid further losses. The panic selling only served to further drive down stock prices, leading to a cascade of selling that eventually led to the steep decline in the Dow Jones Industrial Average.

The market crash of 1987 had a significant impact on the stock market and the broader economy. The decline in stock prices wiped out billions of dollars in wealth and led to a wave of corporate bankruptcies and job losses. It also had a lasting impact on investor psychology, with many investors becoming more cautious and risk-averse in the years that followed.

Managing emotions is an essential aspect of investing. Emotional intelligence refers to the ability to identify, understand, and manage one's emotions effectively. Emotional intelligence is crucial to making sound investment decisions. Investors with high emotional intelligence can manage their emotions effectively, allowing them to make rational investment decisions based on facts rather than emotions.

One of the most effective ways to manage emotions is to develop a disciplined approach to investing. A disciplined approach involves creating a well-defined investment plan and sticking to it, regardless of short-term fluctuations in the market. A disciplined approach helps investors avoid making impulsive decisions based on emotions.

CHAPTER 14. ADVANCED STOCK INVESTING STRATEGIES

"Success in investing doesn't correlate with IQ once you're above the level of 25. Once you have ordinary intelligence, what you need is the temperament to control the urges that get other people into trouble in investing."

Jim Simons

Options trading is an advanced investment strategy that involves buying and selling options contracts. An option is a derivative contract that gives the holder the right, but not the obligation, to buy or sell an underlying asset at a predetermined price and time. Options can be used to hedge against market risks, generate income, or speculate on market movements.

There are two main types of options: call options and put options. A call option gives the holder the right to buy an underlying asset at a predetermined price, known as the strike price, before a specific expiration date. A put option gives the holder the right to sell an underlying asset at a predetermined price, before a specific expiration date. Options can be American style, which can be exercised at any time before the expiration date, or European style, which can only be exercised on the expiration date.

When participating in options trading, one can buy or sell options contracts. If a buyer purchases a call option, they pay a premium to the seller in exchange for the right to purchase an underlying asset at the strike price. If the underlying asset's price rises above the strike price, the buyer can exercise the option and acquire the asset at a lower cost. However, if the price does not increase, the buyer forfeits the premium paid for the option. Similarly, a put option buyer pays a premium to the seller to sell an underlying asset at the strike price. If the price of the asset drops below the strike price, the buyer can exercise the option and sell the asset at a higher price. However, if the price does not decrease, the buyer loses the premium paid for the option.

Investors may enjoy several advantages from trading options. Firstly, options can serve as a hedge against market risks. For instance, an investor who owns a stock but is wary of a possible decrease in price can purchase a put option to protect against this risk. Secondly, options can generate income. By selling options contracts, the seller can generate premium income which could increase portfolio returns. Thirdly, options can be employed to speculate on market movements. Traders may buy or sell options contracts based on their expectations of market fluctuations, potentially profiting from these changes.

There are various risks associated with options trading, making it a high-risk strategy. Firstly, options are considered leveraged instruments, which implies that even a slight move in the underlying asset could cause a significant movement in the option price. Secondly, options come with expiration dates, which necessitates the holder to exercise the option before it expires; otherwise, they risk forfeiting the premium paid for the option. Lastly, engaging in options trading requires an in-depth knowledge of both options and the underlying assets, along with cautious risk management. Investors who do not have a complete understanding of options trading or who do not effectively manage their risks can potentially incur substantial losses.

One of the most famous option trading events occurred in 1995 when a trader at Barings Bank, one of the oldest banks in the UK, lost $1.4 billion in a single day. The trader, Nick Leeson, had been making unauthorized trades in the Singapore futures market, using complex options strategies to bet on the direction of the Nikkei index. However, his bets went sour when the Kobe earthquake struck Japan, causing the Nikkei index to plummet. Leeson was unable to cover his losses and ultimately caused the collapse of Barings Bank, which had been in business for over two centuries.

Another famous option trading event occurred during the financial crisis of 2008 when investors began buying credit default swaps (CDS), a type of option that pays out in the event of a default on a debt instrument. However, as the market for CDS grew, many investors began using them not as a hedge against default risk, but as a way to speculate on the housing market. This led to a dangerous feedback loop, as the rising demand for CDS drove up the cost of insuring against default, which in turn made it harder for homeowners to refinance their mortgages and led to more defaults. Ultimately, the CDS market played a significant role in the financial crisis, as many banks and financial institutions had taken on massive amounts of risk through these options.

A more recent example of option trading in the news is the case of GameStop and the "Reddit rally" of early 2021. A group of retail investors on the social media platform Reddit banded together to buy call options on the struggling video game retailer, which had been heavily shorted by hedge funds. As the stock price rose, the short sellers were forced to buy back their positions, leading to a "short squeeze" and even higher prices. While some individual investors made significant gains from this strategy, others ultimately lost money when the stock price crashed back down. This event illustrated the power of collective action and social media in the world of option trading, but also the risks of speculative trading without a clear understanding of the underlying fundamentals.

Short selling is an advanced stock investing strategy that involves betting against a stock or security in the hopes of profiting from its decline in price. In essence, short sellers borrow shares of a stock from a broker and sell them on the open market, hoping to buy them back at a lower price later and return them to the broker, pocketing the difference as profit.

Investors can benefit from using a particular strategy to hedge their long positions. If an investor owns a stock and is worried about a possible decline in the stock's value, they can use this strategy to mitigate their losses. It involves selling an equal number of shares to the ones owned, thereby lowering their exposure to market downturns and decreasing the overall risk of their portfolio.

Additionally, there is a way to take advantage of market inefficiencies by betting against an overvalued stock or one that is experiencing a temporary price bump. This strategy can result in a profit for investors when the stock returns to its true value.

However, short selling also carries significant risks. For one, losses in short selling can be unlimited since there is no limit to how high a stock's price can rise. If a stock that is shorted starts to rise in price, the short seller must buy back the shares at the higher price to close their position, resulting in a loss.

Another risk of short selling is the potential for a short squeeze. A short squeeze occurs when a stock that is heavily shorted starts to rise in price, leading short sellers to buy back shares to close their positions. If enough short sellers start buying back shares, it can cause the price of the stock to rise rapidly, potentially leading to even greater losses for short sellers who are unable to close their positions quickly enough.

In 2012, hedge fund manager Bill Ackman launched a highly publicized short squeeze attempt against the nutritional supplement company Herbalife. Ackman's hedge fund, Pershing Square Capital Management, took a short position in Herbalife stock, betting that the company's stock price would drop.

Ackman's criticism of Herbalife centered around his belief that the company operated as a pyramid scheme, in which distributors earned money primarily through recruiting new distributors rather than through sales of the company's products. Ackman presented his findings in a widely publicized presentation in December 2012, calling Herbalife "the best-managed pyramid scheme in the history of the world". He also alleged that the company's financials were misleading and that its business model was unsustainable.

In response to Ackman's short position and allegations, Herbalife's management vigorously defended the company and accused Ackman of spreading false information to drive down the company's stock price. The company also launched a public relations campaign to counter Ackman's claims.

As the short squeeze attempt played out over the following months, the price of Herbalife stock became highly volatile. Ackman continued to publicly criticize the company, while Herbalife's stock price rallied on the back of positive earnings reports and increased investor confidence.

In early 2013, other prominent investors, including Carl Icahn, began taking long positions in Herbalife stock, further complicating Ackman's short squeeze attempt. Icahn and Ackman engaged in a public feud over the company, with Icahn accusing Ackman of attempting to manipulate the market and Ackman accusing Icahn of being Herbalife's "enabler".

Despite Ackman's best efforts, the short squeeze attempt ultimately failed. Herbalife's stock price rebounded and continued to rise, frustrating Ackman's bet against the company. In the years since, Herbalife has continued to operate as a publicly traded company, with its stock price remaining volatile and subject to scrutiny from both supporters and critics.

The Herbalife short squeeze attempt by Bill Ackman serves as a cautionary tale for investors seeking to engage in high-profile short selling strategies. While short selling can be a profitable investment technique, it is also a highly risky one that requires careful consideration of both the potential rewards and the potential risks. Additionally, high-profile short squeeze attempts can attract significant attention and scrutiny, potentially leading to unexpected and unwelcome consequences for investors involved.

Another famous short selling event is the case of the Volkswagen Group. In 2008, during the global financial crisis, Volkswagen became the most heavily shorted stock in Europe as investors bet against the company's ability to survive the economic downturn. However, in 2009, the stock price skyrocketed after Porsche, which owned a significant stake in Volkswagen, announced that it had secretly acquired a much larger stake in the company. This led to what is known as a short squeeze, as short sellers were forced to buy shares to cover their positions, driving the price even higher. The Volkswagen short squeeze is considered one of the most significant in history, with some estimates suggesting that short sellers lost over $30 billion.

Margin trading is a popular investing strategy that can be used in conjunction with short selling. By borrowing money from a broker, investors can sell stocks they do not own in the hope of buying them back at a lower price, thereby profiting from the difference. However, margin trading also amplifies potential losses, as investors not only lose money on the price decline of the stocks they sold short, but also have to pay interest on the borrowed funds. In some cases, margin traders may be subject to margin calls, which require them to deposit additional funds or securities to meet their margin requirements.

In margin trading, an investor puts up a portion of the investment's value, known as the margin, and the broker lends the investor the rest of the funds needed to purchase the investment. The amount of margin required varies by broker and by investment, but typically ranges from 25% to 50% of the investment's value. This means that an investor can potentially double their buying power and profits, but they also double their potential losses.

The main advantage of margin trading is the increased buying power it provides. With more money to invest, an investor can potentially generate greater returns than they could with only their own funds. Margin trading can also provide flexibility and allow investors to take advantage of investment opportunities that they might not be able to afford with only their own funds.

Investors who borrow money from a broker to invest in stocks, bonds, or other financial instruments should be aware of the significant risks involved. If the value of the investment declines, the investor may not have enough funds to cover the margin and may be forced to sell at a loss. In addition, interest charges and fees associated with borrowing on margin can reduce potential profits. Furthermore, if an investor is unable to repay the margin, the broker can sell their assets without their consent to cover the debt, resulting in significant losses. It is important to carefully consider the risks before engaging in margin trading.

For experienced individuals who possess a strong comprehension of the risks associated with investing and are knowledgeable about the investments they are pursuing, margin trading can be an effective tool. Nonetheless, it is not advisable for newcomers to investing or those unable to take on substantial financial risks. It is imperative to thoughtfully weigh the potential rewards and hazards of margin trading before implementing this strategy. Additionally, it is recommended to select a trustworthy broker and to fully comprehend the conditions and terms of their margin account.

One famous example of margin trading is the case of the "Nifty Fifty" stocks. In the 1960s and 1970s, the "Nifty Fifty" stocks were considered some of the most reliable and stable investments in the market. These companies were seen as having long-term growth potential and were favored by institutional investors, who poured millions of dollars into them. However, many of these stocks were trading at extremely high price-to-earnings ratios, meaning that investors were willing to pay a premium for their potential growth.

This led to a speculative bubble, with many individual investors using margin trading to purchase shares of the Nifty Fifty stocks. Brokers were eager to lend money to these investors, as the stocks were seen as low-risk investments. However, when the stock market crashed in the early 1970s, many of these investors were unable to cover their margin calls and were forced to sell their shares at a loss. This led to a massive sell-off in the Nifty Fifty stocks, causing their prices to plummet.

One of the most notable casualties of this crash was Xerox, a company that had been one of the most popular Nifty Fifty stocks. Xerox had been trading at an extremely high price-to-earnings ratio of over 40, and many investors had used margin trading to buy shares. When the market crashed, Xerox's stock price fell by over 70%, causing many investors to lose their entire investment.

The Nifty Fifty crash served as a cautionary tale about the dangers of speculative bubbles and margin trading. While it may be tempting to invest in stocks that are seen as low-risk and stable, it is important to carefully consider the risks involved and to avoid overpaying for potential growth. Investors should also be cautious when using margin trading, as it can quickly amplify losses and result in significant financial risk.

CHAPTER 15.
ULTIMATE WINNING
FORMULA

"The stock market is filled with individuals who know the price of everything, but the value of nothing."

Philip Fisher

Over the course of more than 20 years of investing in the stock market, I have developed a winning formula that combines five essential parameters, a valuation method, and a well-calculated ratio. When it comes to these essential parameters, the first one to consider is Return on Invested Capital (ROIC). This financial metric is used to evaluate how effectively a company utilizes its invested capital to generate profits. It is crucial to look at ROIC when valuing a company because it measures how well the company is generating returns on the money it has invested in its business.

In simpler terms, ROIC shows how efficiently a company is using the capital it has available to create value for its shareholders. A high ROIC can indicate that a company has a competitive advantage, while a low ROIC may suggest that a company is not effectively utilizing its resources. As a general rule of thumb, I prefer a ROIC of at least 10% when evaluating a company's financial health. To calculate ROIC, one needs to divide a company's after-tax operating income by the total amount of invested capital, including both debt and equity. The formula is as follows:

ROIC = After-Tax Operating Income / Invested Capital

Invested capital refers to the total amount of money that a company has invested in its business. This includes long-term debt, current debt, and equity. After-tax operating income is the income that a company generates from its operations after accounting for taxes.

A high ROIC indicates that a company is generating significant profits with the capital it has available. A low ROIC, on the other hand, suggests that the company is not using its capital effectively and may not be generating significant returns for its shareholders.

There are several reasons why ROIC is important when valuing a company. First, it provides a clear indication of how effectively a company is using its capital to generate profits. This is crucial because, in the long run, a company that is generating significant returns on its invested capital will be able to create more value for its shareholders than a company that is not.

Second, ROIC can be used to compare companies within the same industry or sector. This allows investors to identify companies that are generating the highest returns on their invested capital and are therefore likely to be the most profitable over the long term.

Third, ROIC can help investors identify companies that are using their capital effectively to invest in growth opportunities. A high ROIC indicates that a company is generating significant returns on its invested capital, which means that it has the ability to reinvest those profits into new growth opportunities and generate even more value for its shareholders.

The second parameter to look for is profit margin. A financial metric that measures the profitability of a company by calculating the amount of profit a company earns for every dollar of revenue it generates. Profit margin is an essential metric to consider when valuing a company because it provides insight into a company's ability to generate profits from its operations.

Profit margin is calculated by dividing a company's net income by its total revenue, expressed as a percentage. For example, if a company has a net income of $10 million and total revenue of $100 million, its profit margin would be 10%. A high profit margin indicates that a company is generating significant profits from its operations, while a low profit margin may suggest that a company is struggling to generate profits.

There are several reasons why profit margin is an important metric to consider when valuing a company. First, profit margin provides insight into a company's pricing power. If a company has a high profit margin, it may be able to charge higher prices for its products or services than its competitors, indicating that it has a competitive advantage. On the other hand, if a company has a low profit margin, it may be struggling to compete on price and may need to cut costs or improve its operations to increase profitability.

Second, profit margin can also indicate a company's efficiency. A company with a high profit margin may be able to generate significant profits while using fewer resources, indicating that it has an efficient business model. Conversely, a company with a low profit margin may be using more resources than necessary to generate profits, indicating that it may need to improve its operations to become more efficient.

Finally, profit margin can also provide insight into a company's financial health. A company with a consistently high profit margin may be in a strong financial position, with the ability to invest in new projects or return capital to shareholders. Conversely, a company with a consistently low profit margin may be in a weaker financial position, with less flexibility to invest in growth initiatives or withstand economic downturns.

The third essential parameter is the current ratio, which assesses a company's ability to meet its short-term liabilities with its current assets. It is calculated by dividing a company's current assets by its current liabilities. A higher current ratio generally indicates that a company is more capable of meeting its short-term financial obligations.

The importance of the current ratio in valuing a company lies in the fact that it provides insights into a company's liquidity and ability to manage its short-term financial obligations. A high current ratio suggests that a company has enough cash and other liquid assets to pay off its debts in the near future without relying on external financing, while a low current ratio may indicate that the company is struggling to meet its financial obligations and may face cash flow problems.

Investors and analysts often use the current ratio as one of several metrics to assess a company's financial health and determine its overall value. For example, if a company has a current ratio of 2, it means that it has twice as many current assets as current liabilities, suggesting that it is in a strong financial position. On the other hand, if a company has a current ratio of less than 1, it means that it has more current liabilities than current assets, which could be a sign of financial trouble.

The current ratio is especially important in industries where companies must regularly meet short-term financial obligations, such as retail or manufacturing. These companies often rely on a steady flow of cash to fund their operations, and a low current ratio could indicate that the company may have difficulty paying off debts or purchasing inventory.

In addition to using the current ratio to assess a company's financial health, investors may also use it to compare companies within the same industry or sector. For example, if Company A has a current ratio of 2 and Company B has a current ratio of 1, it suggests that Company A may be in a stronger financial position than Company B.

The free cash flow to debt ratio (FCF/Debt) is the fourth crucial metric used to evaluate the financial health of a company. This ratio provides insight into a company's ability to repay its debts using its available cash flows.

Free cash flow (FCF) is the amount of cash generated by a company after accounting for capital expenditures, working capital, and taxes. This measure represents the amount of cash that is available for distribution to shareholders, debt repayment, and investments in new projects. On the other hand, debt refers to the amount of money that a company has borrowed from lenders and must repay over time.

The FCF/Debt ratio is calculated by dividing a company's free cash flow by its outstanding debt. This ratio provides a valuable indicator of a company's ability to manage its debt obligations with its existing cash flows. Essentially, the higher the ratio, the more cash a company has available to service its debt, which is an indication of its financial strength.

In the valuation process, investors look for companies that have a high FCF/Debt ratio as it indicates the company is generating enough cash flow to cover its debt obligations. A high FCF/Debt ratio means that a company has enough cash to cover its interest payments and principal repayments without straining its financial resources. This is important because it demonstrates the company's ability to withstand market downturns, economic slowdowns, and other unforeseen events that can impact a company's financial performance.

On the other hand, a low FCF/Debt ratio may signal that a company is in financial distress and could struggle to meet its debt obligations. This could be a warning sign to investors to proceed with caution or to avoid the company altogether. A low

FCF/Debt ratio could also indicate that the company is taking on too much debt relative to its cash flow, which could lead to financial problems down the road.

This ratio is particularly important when valuing companies with a significant amount of debt. High debt levels can increase a company's financial risk and make it more vulnerable to market downturns. By assessing a company's FCF/Debt ratio, investors can gain a better understanding of the company's financial health and make informed decisions about whether or not to invest.

While there are many metrics to consider when evaluating a company's financial performance and potential for future growth, earnings per share (EPS) growth is undoubtedly one of the last metrics I would suggest overlooking. In particular, the projected EPS growth rate for the next 10 years is a crucial aspect of this metric, as it provides valuable insight into a company's long-term earnings potential.

EPS is calculated by dividing a company's net income by its outstanding shares of common stock. EPS growth measures the rate at which a company's earnings per share are increasing or decreasing over time. Projected EPS growth over the next 10 years is an estimate of the rate at which a company's earnings per share are expected to grow in the future. This estimate is typically based on various factors, such as historical earnings growth rates, industry trends, and future growth prospects.

The projected EPS growth rate over the next 10 years is a crucial factor in determining the value of a company's stock. Investors use this metric to evaluate a company's long-term profitability and to estimate the potential returns on their investment. Companies with high projected EPS growth rates over the next decade are typically viewed as more attractive investment opportunities than those with low or negative projected EPS growth rates. Short-term fluctuations in earnings are common, but projecting EPS growth over a 10-year period can help investors gain a better understanding of a company's underlying financial strength and future prospects. Companies with consistently high projected EPS growth rates over the next decade are likely to have a strong competitive position in their industry, with a solid track record of innovation and growth.

Another benefit of using projected EPS growth over the next 10 years in valuing a company is that it can help investors compare different companies within the same industry. By looking at the projected EPS growth rates of different companies, investors can determine which companies are likely to outperform their peers and which ones may be lagging behind. This information can be particularly valuable for investors looking to build a diversified portfolio of stocks.

When it comes to valuation, I have found that the most accurate method is calculating a company's value based on its ability to generate future cash flows. To determine the value of a stock, one must estimate the future cash flows that the company is expected to generate and discount those cash flows to their present value.

To estimate future cash flows, it's best to examine the company's historical earnings and project future earnings based on its growth rate. I recommend using a 10-year period to project future earnings and caution against overly optimistic growth rate estimates. To confirm my growth rate calculation, I usually look for patterns in historic revenue growth and profit margin behavior.

After projecting future earnings, the next step is to calculate the present value of those earnings using a discount rate. The discount rate is the rate of return that an investor requires to invest in the stock. To reflect the risks associated with investing in the stock market, it's recommended to use a discount rate that incorporates the risk-free rate, typically around 10%.

I recommend using the discounted cash flow (DCF) method to calculate the present value of future earnings. The DCF method involves multiplying each year's projected earnings by a discount factor, which is calculated as (1 + discount rate) raised to the power of the number of years in the future. The sum of these discounted future earnings represents the present value of the stock.

It's also a good recommendation to adjust the present value of the stock based on the company's current financial situation. For instance, if the company has a significant amount of debt, subtracting the value of the debt from the present value of the stock is advisable. After calculating the present value of the stock, compare it to its current market price. If the calculated value is significantly higher than the market price, the stock may be undervalued and represent a good investment opportunity. It's recommended to have a margin of safety of at least 30%.

Now, in my experience, the PEG ratio is one of the best metrics for evaluating stocks. This ratio combines a company's price-to-earnings (P/E) ratio with its expected earnings growth rate and dividend yield. Legendary investor Peter Lynch was a proponent of using the PEG ratio, and for good reason. By looking at a stock's PEG ratio, investors can identify undervalued companies with strong growth prospects. This makes it a powerful tool for any investor looking to build a successful investment portfolio.

The P/E ratio is a common valuation metric used by investors to evaluate a company's financial performance. It is calculated by dividing a company's stock price by its earnings per share (EPS). However, the P/E ratio alone does not give investors a complete picture of a company's value. This is where the PEG ratio comes in.

The PEG ratio is a financial metric that divides a company's P/E ratio by its expected earnings growth rate and dividend yield, providing investors with a more complete picture of its value. A PEG ratio of less than 1 suggests that a stock may be undervalued and could present a good investment opportunity, while a PEG ratio of more than 1 suggests that a stock may be overvalued and could potentially be a bad investment. When using the PEG ratio, I typically recommend a margin of safety of at least 50%, and would only consider investing in a stock with a PEG ratio of 0.5 or less.

Peter Lynch, a former manager of the Fidelity Magellan Fund, believed that a company's expected growth rate and dividend yield were crucial factors in determining its value. He argued that investors should not just focus on a company's current earnings, but also consider its growth potential and its ability to pay dividends. By factoring in a company's growth potential and dividend yield, the PEG ratio can help investors identify stocks that are undervalued or overvalued based on their growth potential and ability to pay dividends.

One of the stocks that he famously bought using the PEG ratio as a base for his purchase is the specialty retailer, The Limited, that operated in the women's clothing and accessories space. The company was founded in 1963 by Leslie Wexner and was known for its innovative approach to retailing. The Limited was known for its ability to quickly identify fashion trends and bring them to market at an affordable price point.

In the early 1980s, Lynch identified The Limited as an attractive investment opportunity. At the time, The Limited was a relatively unknown retailer with a market capitalization of just $250 million. However, Lynch saw potential in the company's unique business model and strong growth prospects. He used the PEG ratio to determine that the stock was undervalued, with a PEG ratio of just 0.5, well below the industry average of 1.0.

In 1980, Lynch initiated a position in The Limited, purchasing 600,000 shares at an average price of $1.75 per share. Over the next several years, The Limited's stock price soared as the company continued to experience strong growth. By 1990, The Limited's stock price had reached $45 per share, resulting in a return of over 2,500% for Lynch and his investors.

Lynch's investment in The Limited is a classic example of his investment philosophy in action. He believed that individual investors could achieve great success by carefully researching and analyzing potential investments, focusing on companies with strong growth prospects, and using valuation metrics like the PEG ratio to determine whether a stock was undervalued.

ABOUT THE AUTHOR

JACK FISHER is a former engineer, entrepreneur, and investor. He lives in California, United States with his fiancé and two children. Jack loves educating and inspiring other investors and entrepreneurs to succeed and live the life of their dreams.